D1525177

FREEDOM
THROUGH
MILITARY VICTORY

R. B. THIEME, JR.

R. B. THIEME, JR., BIBLE MINISTRIES

HOUSTON, TEXAS

This book is edited from the lectures and unpublished notes of R. B. Thieme, Jr.

A catalogue of available tapes and publications will be provided upon request.

R. B. Thieme, Jr., Bible Ministries
P. O. Box 460829, Houston, Texas 77056-8829
www.rbthieme.org

Printed in the United States of America

ISBN 1-55764-061-0

Dedication

IN 1756 MAJOR ROBERT ROGERS ORGANIZED among the Continentals nine companies of Rangers who served with great distinction in the French and Indian War. Rogers' Rangers began one of the oldest and finest traditions in the United States Army—a legacy of military excellence, a reputation for supreme courage. This tradition has endured throughout the military history of our nation.

Rangers have served with distinction from the Battle of Bloody Ridge in 1763 and the Battle of Cowpens in 1781 to the eighteen days of Chiunizi Pass, Anzio, Cisterna; the landings on Omaha Beach, Normandy; Task Force Sugar, Leyte, Luzon; Myitkyina Air Field, Burma; the Yalu River, North Korea; Vietnam; Grenada; Desert Storm; Somalia.

In October 1951, the Chief of Staff, Gen. J. Lawton Collins, authorized the Commandant of the Infantry School at Fort Benning, Georgia, to establish a Ranger Department for the purpose of perpetuating this outstanding military training in the United States Army.

In 1971 the Ranger Department added a new tradition: a class of Reserve Officer Training Corps cadets. This book is dedicated to the first ROTC Ranger Class in United States Army history, Class 502-71. Highly motivated and tested to the limit physically, mentally, and psychologically, this class received the toughest training from the finest officer and noncommissioned officer personnel in the Army.

On 12 August 1971 at Fort Benning, Georgia, my son, Ranger Robert B. Thieme III, was a graduating member of that first ROTC class—a testimony to the grace of God and to the application of Bible doctrine.

R. B. Thieme, Jr.

Editor's Note

FREEDOM THROUGH MILITARY VICTORY was written for two purposes. The first is to delineate the biblical principle that freedom depends on a strong military organization standing ready to defend and to protect its citizens and borders from the aggression of external enemies. No nation can survive the destruction of its military. The second is a corollary of the first. Since the military is biblically sanctioned to preserve freedom, the Christian has a responsibility to serve his country as a soldier and to support the military as a civilian.

This book is a revision of the 1971 edition of *Freedom through Military Victory* combined with the 1990 transcript *In Harm's Way*. Pertinent principles were also extracted from related out-of-print books by R. B. Thieme, Jr., including *The Christian Warrior* (1975), *Divine Establishment* (1988), *National Crisis* (1971), and *War: Moral or Immoral?* (1974).

Respect for the military as a cornerstone of divine establishment is reflected in the ministry of R. B. Thieme, Jr. His service during World War II and the memory of comrades-in-arms who died defending freedom have infused a personal appreciation of the subject onto the pages of this book. His ministry has influenced countless believers both to serve their nation as a soldier and the Lord Jesus Christ as a Christian warrior.

R. B. Thieme III

To Those Who Serve

While living on an army post, as I did during World War II, there were three events that always impressed me. These were military traditions that influenced my motivation and contributed to a desire to serve my country.

First was the "wake-up" call. Reveille always meant responsibility and privilege. Each morning when the bugle sounded I was reminded of my dedication to serve my country another day.

Second, I could hear the boom of the sunset gun followed by the bugle playing "To the Colors." As the flag was being lowered, everywhere everything stopped. Men got out of their cars and all came to attention. Facing the direction of the flagpole, which we could not see, we stood at attention until the last sound of the bugle faded away. Our salute was a reminder that the flag represented something more important than we were.

Third, "lights out" in the barracks was followed by the sounding of the bugle rendering those poignant notes of "Taps." A duty day had ended and we had been part of a military organization that had a mission. We were not important, but our mission was. We had the privilege of being a part of a team. We merged our personalities into something more important than we were. Briefly I reflected on the day's activities and then fell asleep.

Each of these three daily events on a military post was a reminder to me that dedication to military service is the basis for freedom through military victory. Then as now I remember Philippians 1:21.

For me living, Christ; dying, profit.

And so it is in the ministry. Now I am dedicated to the Lord's service, to teaching the Word of God to you. Now I wake up to a different reveille—Bible doctrine in my soul. In the darkness of the night I often find myself awake thinking doctrine—thinking about things that I'm preparing to present to you as part of my service to the Lord. Now my bugle sound is my typewriter and my day on post is centered around one mission—to extrapolate and teach biblical truth.

My standard is always the same—Bible doctrine is far more important than I am.

> You have magnified Your word above and beyond Your
> name. (Ps. 138:2*b*)

These prophetic words written by David about our Lord Jesus Christ signify the standard raised for those who serve. Daily I salute this standard raised for all Christian soldiers by the humanity of Jesus Christ in the dispensation of the hypostatic union. He has given every Church Age believer the option of following the colors to the high ground of spiritual maturity and glorifying God during that time between salvation through faith in Christ and the end of our time here on earth which I call "Taps."

Evening "Taps" sounds for me only after I accomplish my mission by teaching with accuracy the Word of God as I seek to do night after night. And when my final "Taps" is sounded and the Lord decides to take me home, God will decide the time, the manner, and the place of my death. For me death has lost its sting; the grave has lost its power and I can say when my head goes down for that last time, "Thanks be to God who gives us the victory through our Lord Jesus Christ."

I salute you for your dedication to the military and to our Lord. You provide the freedom for me to continue to study and teach.

Vincit omnia veritas,

L/Col., USAF-Ret.
26 December 1996

Contents

Part Two: To the Soldier

Glossary

Indices

Preface

Before you begin your Bible study, if you are a believer in the Lord Jesus Christ, be sure you have named your sins privately to God the Father.

> If we confess our [known] sins, He is faithful and righteous to forgive us our [known] sins and to cleanse us from all [unknown, or forgotten sins] unrighteousness. (1 John 1:9)

You will then be in fellowship with God, filled with the Holy Spirit, and ready to learn Bible doctrine from the Word of God.

> "God is spirit, and those who worship Him must worship in [the filling of the] spirit and [biblical] truth." (John 4:24)

If you have never personally believed in the Lord Jesus Christ as your Savior, the issue is not naming your sins. The issue is faith alone in Christ alone.

> "He who believes in the Son has eternal life; but he who does not obey [the command to believe in] the Son shall not see life, but the wrath of God abides on him." (John 3:36)

THE WORD OF GOD is alive and powerful, sharper than any two-edged sword, piercing even to the dividing asunder of the soul and the spirit, and of the joints and the marrow, and is a critic of thoughts and intents of the heart. (Heb. 4:12)

All Scripture is God-breathed, and is profitable for doctrine, for reproof, for correction, for instruction in righteousness; that the man of God might be mature, thoroughly furnished unto all good works. (2 Tim. 3:16–17)

Study to show thyself approved unto God, a workman that needeth not to be ashamed, rightly dividing the word of truth. (2 Tim. 2:15)

Part One

TO THE NATION

What Price Freedom

BELLIGERENT NATIONS WIELD MILITARY FORCE not to defend their sovereignty but to vanquish and enslave other nations. Is resistance to such aggression worth the price of young men marching to war? Each generation must decide. If a nation wishes to perpetuate as inviolate the priceless privileges and blessings of independence, warfare is inevitable. Every generation must face the crucible of war. Freedom is bought and paid for by the blood of individuals who set a higher value on their liberty than on life itself. If one generation is not prepared mentally and spiritually to defend such values, if enough individuals in a national entity reject the principle of freedom through military victory, liberty languishes.

Despite man's zealous efforts to achieve freedom through peaceful means, wars will continue until the end of human history when Jesus Christ, the "Prince of Peace," reigns on earth for one thousand years (Isa. 9:6; cf., Eccl. 3:8; Micah 4:1–3; Mark 13:7; Rev. 20:4). For man to presume that he can accomplish what only Jesus Christ can accomplish in the Millennium is a total disregard for the Scriptures and the height of arrogance. Jesus Himself declared the certainty of war.

> "And you will be hearing of wars [armed conflict] and rumors of wars [cold wars]; see that you are not frightened, for *those things* must take place [a part of history], but *that* is not yet the end [of the Tribulation]. For nation will

rise against nation, and kingdom against kingdom." (Matt.
24:6–7*a*) [1]

Only when Jesus Christ inaugurates His kingdom at the Second Advent will warfare be abolished.

Until then conflict, a manifestation of the sin nature resident in every person and Satan's rulership of this world (John 12:31), will plague mankind. The fate of nations will continue to be decided on the battlefields of the world. A nation must prepare for war to ensure an endowment of freedom and an interim of peace.

> A time to kill, and a time to heal;
> A time to tear down, and a time to build up. . . .
> A time for war, and a time for peace. (Eccl. 3:3, 8*b*)

In A.D. 425 Augustine, Bishop of Hippo and antiquity's foremost theologian, affirmed the biblical principle of freedom through military victory in his letters to Boniface, chief warlord of the western Roman Empire. Augustine exhorted Boniface to defend Mauretania, a Roman colony in north Africa, against the invading Vandals. Augustine reassured his Christian friend that he could serve in the military, slay the enemy, and still glorify God.

> Some, then, in praying for you [Boniface], fight against your invisible enemies; you, in fighting for them, contend against the Barbarians, their visible enemies. . . . Think, then, of this first of all, when you are arming for the battle, that even your bodily strength is a gift of God. . . . War is waged in order that peace may be obtained. [2]

Peace is the ideal environment for freedom. Freedom is exemption from arbitrary, external control, the function of free will uncoerced by

---

1. R. B. Thieme, Jr., *The Divine Outline of History: Dispensations and the Church* (Houston: R. B. Thieme, Jr., Bible Ministries, 1989), 72–75; and Thieme, *Anti-Semitism* (2003), 102, 106. Hereafter, cross-references to my books will cite only author, title, date of publication (in the first reference), and page(s).

All Scriptures in this book are quoted from the New American Standard Bible (NASB). Bracketed commentary reflects amplification of the NASB translation taught in Bible class lectures (available on tape from R. B. Thieme, Jr., Bible Ministries, Houston, Texas).

2. Philip Schaff, ed., *Nicene and Post-Nicene Fathers of the Christian Church*, 14 vols., first series (Grand Rapids: William B. Eerdmans Publishing Co., 1983), 1:553–54.

threat or violence. For a client nation to God like the United States of America, Bible doctrine in the soul of believers is the foundation for freedom (John 8:32).[3]

> And I will walk at liberty [in freedom],
> For I seek Thy precepts [Bible doctrine]. (Ps. 119:45)

The pursuit of biblical truth always promotes personal and national freedom. Yet maintaining that freedom demands a strong national defense—a military establishment trained, motivated, and supported to defend national freedom and interests.

The Constitution and Bill of Rights of the United States of America define our liberty. Yet these cherished fundamentals of American government would have been worthless parchment without the six-and-a-half year war in which the Continental army defeated the tyranny enforced by the British army. Today, the U.S. military still defends and preserves our precious freedom from eradication by foreign enemies. Only armies can protect freedom from armies that seek to destroy freedom. The United States, or any nation that desires autonomy, must maintain a military force trained and equipped for war.

The United States faces an impasse! During the twentieth century our foreign policy was one of intermittent isolationism resulting in drastic military reduction, especially between the world wars and after the fiasco of Vietnam and the victory of Desert Storm. Such a policy assumes that insulating this country from foreign conflicts will secure freedom and peace. But when bellicose nations pursue confrontation, a policy of isolationism and disarmament is divorced from reality.

As the United States emerged from a period of isolationism preceding 1939, the handwriting on the wall spelled war. The United States sought peace but Germany and Japan would not be deterred from their course of conflagration. Our lack of military preparedness and policy of appeasement inevitably drew us into World War II. A generation of soldiers paid a terrible price for our weakness. Yet those who fought and won that war understood and abided by the principles of divine establishment. They crushed the enemy and ensured freedom for their generation.

---

3. Thieme, *The Divine Outline of History*, 35–37, 67–69; see also "The Client Nation," page 16.

The freedom the United States possesses has been purchased through the sacrifice and suffering of courageous men. We as a people have the right of self-determination because of military victory. We as Christians have the privilege to assemble in public worship services and to evangelize unbelievers without persecution courtesy of the military. Since 1776, we owe an immeasurable debt to all our gallant fighting forces, especially to those who gave their lives that we might remain a free people. To sustain our liberty the people of the United States of America must observe the laws of divine establishment.

LAWS OF DIVINE ESTABLISHMENT

In His omniscience God knew in eternity past that man would choose to sin. He knew that once man acquired a sin nature he would have unlimited potential to destroy himself. To preserve and perpetuate human existence during the course of the angelic conflict,[4] God instituted the laws of divine establishment for believer and unbeliever—principles designed for the protection, stability, orderly function, survival, and blessing of the human race. These laws declare freedom to be man's most valuable possession. When mankind observes these laws, he restrains the sin nature and exhibits the highest expression of individual freedom.

The human race cannot long endure without a system of control. Legitimate authority, the umbrella of divine establishment, protects human freedom. Authority is the power delegated by God through the laws of divine establishment whereby certain members of the human race have responsibility for and jurisdiction over other members of the human race. Authority protects self-determination, privacy, property, human life—the basic components of freedom. While authority exists in both the spiritual and temporal realms, divine establishment involves only temporal authority.

An example of divine establishment is the Ten Commandments ordained exclusively to govern the theocratic client nation of Israel. This "Magna Carta" of human freedom defined liberty, morality, and divine

---

4. The angelic conflict is the unseen warfare between God and Satan, ignited by the prehistoric revolt of Satan and one-third of the angels, that continues as spiritual warfare in human history. Thieme, *Christian Integrity* (2002), 14.

authority for believers and unbelievers within Israel. The first five commandments embodied the sovereign rule of *Yahweh* over the national entity and served as an evangelistic witness to the unbeliever. For believers in Israel these commandments defined individual spiritual freedom and provided the environment for developing a spiritual life (Ex. 20:1–12; cf., John 8:32), but did not constitute the spiritual life. The last five formed the biblical paradigm for morality and summarized the hallowed precepts of civil independence that protect the privacy and property of believers and unbelievers alike (Ex. 20:13–17). Although this code was designed by God specifically for Israel, these same truths guarantee personal freedom and national liberty to any nation operating under divine establishment axioms.[5]

THE DIVINE INSTITUTIONS

God ordained four divine institutions through which the laws of divine establishment function: the individual, marriage, family, and the national entity. These four founding principles for mankind are clearly delineated and consistently verified by Scripture. God delegated a primary authority within each institution: volition for the individual, the husband for marriage, parents for the family, and government for the national entity. While the divine institutions were in God's plan from eternity past, they came into existence at various points of time. The individual was ordained with the creation of Adam in Genesis 1:26;

Divine Institution	Authority from Divine Establishment
1. The Individual	1. Volition
2. Marriage	2. Husband
3. Family	3. Parents
4. The National Entity	4. Government

5. Thieme, *The Divine Outline of History*, 32–35, 56–64.

marriage with the creation of the woman in Genesis 2:22; family with
the birth of the first child in Genesis 4:1; the national entity with the
formation of nations in Genesis 10:5. These four institutions apply to
every human being regardless of race, nationality, gender, social or
spiritual status, or any other factor.

The Individual

Adam was originally created perfect by God as a trichotomous
individual—a composite of body, soul, and spirit.[6] When he disobeyed
God and sinned, Adam became dichotomous—body and soul. At the
Fall he lost the human spirit and acquired a sin nature, the source of
spiritual death. As his progeny, every human being is born dichotomous and spiritually dead, unable to have fellowship with God (Rom.
5:12). Regeneration by faith alone in Jesus Christ alone creates anew
the human spirit, rendering the believer in Christ trichotomous and
spiritually alive.

The basic authority for the first divine institution is volition. God
created man to operate rationally under the volition in his soul rather
than according to his instincts. While there is variation in human apti-
tude and capacity to learn, all individuals possess this decision-making
ability. God could have computerized the human race so that individuals would be programmed to carry out His plan. Instead, He
desires that every person respond to His grace and serve Him willingly
without coercion.

Mandates from God are directed toward volition. Therefore, volition
is a major issue in the angelic conflict; everyone must be a free agent to
accept or reject eternal salvation and then to serve Him (Josh. 24:15).

> "He who believes in the Son [Jesus Christ] has eternal
> life; but he who does not obey [the mandate to believe in]
> the Son shall not see life, but the wrath of God abides on
> him." (John 3:36)

> Who [God] desires all men to be saved and to come to the
> [full] knowledge of the truth. (1 Tim. 2:4)

---

6. Thieme, *The Barrier* (1993), 8–10, 15; *Heathenism* (2001), 9.

Proper regulation of volition in the soul of both believers and unbelievers demands self-discipline. Self-discipline is the consistent decision to do what ought to be done with the determination to avoid any distractions that hinder the accomplishment of an objective. This fundamental character trait is a foundation for integrity, honor, and nobility, as well as all other virtuous attributes that enable each person to fulfill his destiny. Without self-discipline man abuses freedom by making bad decisions. Truly great people in life are self-disciplined.

One of Robert E. Lee's lieutenant generals, John Brown Gordon, described the importance of self-discipline to personal character and national freedom. He tells the story of Confederate troops in June of 1862 facing an almost invincible Union position on the summit of Malvern Hill during the Seven Days' Battles around Richmond, Virginia. Northern artillery was mercilessly pounding the Southern lines, tearing huge gaps through the ranks. As shells struck, the victims were literally blown apart. Noise, dust, and death enveloped the embattled troops. In the midst of this carnage a panic-stricken rabbit suddenly darted from its hiding place and sprinted furiously toward the rear, away from the gunfire. A mountaineer in the Confederate ranks, noting the rabbit's speed and direction of flight, raised his voice above the din of battle and shouted, "Go to it, Molly Cottontail! I'd be going with you if it wasn't for my character!"

General Gordon continued:

In this connection, I am reminded of the commonplace but important truth that the aggregate character of a people of any country depends upon the personal character of its individual citizens; and that the stability of the popular government depends far more upon the character, the individual, personal character of its people, than it does upon any Constitution that could be adopted or statutes that could be enacted. What would safeguards be worth if the character of the people did not sustain and enforce them? The Constitution would be broken, the laws defied; riot and anarchy would destroy both, and with them the government itself. I am not assuming or suggesting that this country is in any present danger of such an experience; but of all the countries on earth this one, with its universal suffrage, its divergent and conflicting interests, its immense expanse of territory, and its large population, made up from every class and clime, and still to be increased in the coming years, is far more dependent than any other upon the character of its people.[7]

Today, General Gordon's words ring prophetic. The decisions you make manifest your character, integrity, and wisdom and determine the course of your life and the stability of your nation. When the majority of citizens in a nation decide to shun establishment principles, the balance between authority and freedom ceases to exist. Remember: Freedom without authority is anarchy and authority without freedom is tyranny. Achieving the proper balance between freedom and authority demands a personal sense of responsibility. With the freedom to make decisions comes the responsibility for the repercussions of those decisions.

One dimension of divine establishment is the law of volitional responsibility which stipulates that you are accountable for your own decisions and actions. Hence you can never blame others for the mishaps and suffering that result from your bad decisions. You must take full responsibility for your associations, activities, motives, and modus operandi.

People have the ability to exercise freedom of choice to determine the course of their lives, unless severely limited by some form of tyranny or slavery. Yet not even the cruelest tyranny can remove what you choose to think. If you are free and decide to operate under divine establishment precepts, you sustain and preserve your personal freedom. If you decide to reject these divine precepts, you progressively limit your future options. The choices you make dictate the life you lead.

Marriage

After salvation one of the most important decisions in life is that of a lifetime partner. Marriage and volition originated in the Garden of Eden before the Fall (Gen. 2:22–24). Since the man and the woman must make a decision to enter this mutual relationship, marriage is an application of the authority of the first divine institution. Marriage provides the structure for stability in society, the foundation of civilization. God's plan for husband and wife prohibits fornication, adultery, promiscuity,

---

7. John B. Gordon, *Reminiscences of the Civil War* (New York: Charles Scribner's Sons, 1904), 76–77.

homosexuality, communal living, polygamy, and frivolous divorce. When the divine design for marriage is spurned by enough people, degeneracy permeates society and the nation declines.

God designed one specific man for one specific woman. He assigns authority to the husband (Eph. 5:22–23; Col. 3:18; 1 Pet. 3:1) who is mandated to love his wife (Eph. 5:25) and to assume the responsibility to guard and maintain her freedom. To fulfill his obligation, the husband must possess and express from his soul virtue, honor, and integrity. The woman must also possess virtue in her soul. She is mandated to "respect" the authority of her husband (Eph. 5:33*b*) to whom she willingly surrenders her freedom. This respect is the highest form of a woman's love in marriage.

The marriage of the right man to the right woman:

1. Forms the most basic unit in society;
2. Provides the framework for conjugal love and the only legitimate environment for sex;
3. Becomes the foundation for the third divine institution—the family.

Family

This fundamental organization of society combines with marriage to form a second biblical safeguard for the perpetuation of the human race. Two parents, mother and father, create the environment for raising children. An infant enters the world helpless, needing protection and training until able to sustain himself. The family offers material provision, security, discipline, and guidance enveloped in parental love.

In addition to these staples of nurturing, parents are mandated to instill in their children norms and standards. Authority in the family is vested in the parents. Parents must teach children obedience, the difference between right and wrong, and inculcate them with the principles of self-discipline, manners, and respect for others. Training and correction within the family convey stability to the individual, as well as to the national entity.

> And, fathers, do not provoke your children to anger; but bring them up in the discipline and instruction of the Lord. (Eph. 6:4)

While parents have numerous responsibilities, children have only one responsibility within the family—to respect and obey their parents (Eph. 6:1–3).

"Honor your father and your mother, that your days may be prolonged in the land [nation] which the LORD your God gives you." (Ex. 20:12)

He who curses his father or his mother,
His lamp will go out [death] in time of darkness.
    (Prov. 20:20)

The eye that mocks a father,
And scorns a mother,
The ravens of the valley will pick it out,
And the young eagles will eat it. (Prov. 30:17)

Once a child learns to obey his parents and understands the principle of authority, he is prepared to respect all other authorities in life, including those appointed over him in a military organization.

When basic principles of authority and self-discipline are not taught early in a child's life, they often reject all forms of authority as teenagers and young adults. Without authority orientation taught in the home that includes personal humility and respect for adult supervision, juveniles become insolent and defiant. Devoid of boundaries and self-absorbed, they reject divine establishment norms and standards. Peer pressure replaces adult authority. Self-gratification replaces the authority of law. These young people turn to alcohol abuse, illegal drugs, illicit sex, or gang activity. Violence becomes rampant, criminality is commonplace. If a significant number of young people defy authority, mindless rebellion overwhelms an entire generation.

When parents do not fulfill their responsibility and children do not "honor" their parents, the nation suffers from insecurity, instability, and eventual loss of liberty. National disintegration begins in the family.

1. Insecure husbands result in insecure wives.
2. Insecure parents result in insecure children.
3. Insecure children produce an insecure generation.
4. An insecure generation demands security.
5. In demanding security from government an insecure generation becomes an entitlement generation.

6. Entitlements are offered to an insecure generation by insecure politicians.

7. Insecure politicians offer some form of socialism that is always divorced from establishment principles found in the infallible Word of God.

8. An insecure government gains power and entitlements for itself and finances the pseudosecurity of socialism through confiscation of wealth by unjust taxation and redistribution of wealth in the name of the greater good for the greater number.

9. Utopian socialism combines with Marxism to establish economic and political doctrines based on false theories of dialectical materialism and the promotion of class warfare. The result is a demagogic government that offers pseudosecurity to an insecure generation through public lies and false promises, destroying individual and national freedom.

10. Instead of government being the servant of the people, the entitled, insecure people become slaves to a dictatorial bureaucracy. Absolute power in the hands of insecure and incompetent rulers whose power lust feeds on an insecure generation demanding something for nothing results in a nation selling its heritage of freedom for a mess of pottage.

The cycle of insecurity starts with the dissolution of the family and ends with the internal self-destruction of a nation. Therefore, maintaining stability and freedom depend on the integrity and standards of marital and parental authority. When parents have no virtue, the next generation lacks virtue, becomes insecure, and the nation declines.

The National Entity

Evil was rampant throughout the world during the age of negative volition (Gen. 6:1–7). So God took severe measures to insure the survival of the human race by precipitating the worldwide Flood.[8] After the Flood only Noah's family survived; they alone expressed faith in the Savior and remained true to His plan. From Noah's sons, Shem, Ham, and Japheth, sprang three groups of gentile descendants, all of

---

8. Thieme, *The Divine Outline of History*, 25–27.

whom spoke the same language (Gen. 11:1). As the population increased, eventually they gathered at Babel in a satanically inspired rebellion against God. They presumed to "*reach* into heaven" through
their own ability and concerted effort.

The city of Babel was to become a world center for the human race
with the monumental tower to serve as a physical and spectacular
symbol of world unification.[9]

> And they said, "Come, let us build for ourselves a city
> [Babel], and a tower whose top *will reach* into heaven,
> and let us make for ourselves a name; lest we be scattered
> abroad over the face of the whole earth." (Gen. 11:4)

Human achievement although sometimes admirable often has evil
consequences. When human accomplishments obscure the reality of
man's total separation from God or supplant the grace of God as the
one true solution to human problems, God intervenes. Divine judgment at Babel confounded the language of the people and divided
them into various nations.

> Therefore its name was called Babel, because there the
> LORD confused the language of the whole earth; and from
> there the LORD scattered them abroad over the face of the
> whole earth. (Gen. 11:9)

Bible scholars have observed and commented on the political and
cultural impact of God's action at Babel.

> The nature of the divine judgment upon this first try at a World
> State is deeply interesting. It is generally conceded that the ce-
> ment which holds men together in groups and nations is what
> we call a common culture, and the very core of such a culture is
> found in language, man's marvelous ability to communicate
> ideas. It was exactly at this point that the judgment of God
> struck: the common bond of "one language" was supernaturally
> destroyed [Gen. 11:6–7], and the multiplication of tongues led
> to the formation of different groups and, ultimately, nations. For
> the chief obstacle to the achievement of the one world state of
> "Internationalism," . . . is the barrier of language.[10]

---

9. Alva J. McClain, *The Greatness of the Kingdom* (Winona Lake: BMH Books, 1959), 47.
10. Ibid., 48–49.

God's judgment upon this one-world government was a clear warning against all efforts to establish any form of international rule and a ringing endorsement for the concept of the national entity. In a world dominated by the sin nature, absolute power vested in a unified international body would always degenerate into ironclad totalitarianism.

To protect the human race from the self-destructiveness of a one-world state God established the national entity as the fourth divine institution. He "scattered" mankind to limit the expression of human arrogance and impede the spread of evil (Gen. 11:8). The division was originally based on racial, geographic, and linguistic boundaries.

> From these the coastlands of the nations were separated into their lands [geography], every one according to his language, according to their families [race], into their nations. (Gen. 10:5)

If everyone in the world spoke the same language, wickedness would intensify. Different languages and the founding of the client nation to God constitute a divine barrier against the proliferation of evil.

The Apostle Paul's address to the Athenians establishes the validity of the fourth divine institution for the Church Age, allowing Christians to apply the ancient lesson from Babel to the current dispensation. Paul emphasizes that God's purpose in separating the nations and setting "the boundaries of their habitation" is "that they should seek God" rather than be inordinately impressed with human achievement embodied in the religion, philosophy, and poetry of the Greeks (Acts 17:26–27; cf., 17:21, 23, 28).

National entities exist to prevent the world from degenerating into chaos. God sanctions nations to restrain man's sin nature. They provide a deterrent against the tyranny Satan seeks to perpetrate on the human race and the lethal tendencies of mankind. God also sanctions government as the authority within a national entity to restrain the unbridled evil that man without boundaries will commit. Government is designed to protect individual volition, safeguard privacy and property, and maintain internal tranquillity through law enforcement and external security through military preparedness (1 Pet. 2:13–14).

> Let every person be in subjection to the governing authorities. For there is no authority except from God, and those which exist are established by God. Therefore he

who resists authority has opposed the ordinance of God;
and they who have opposed will receive condemnation
upon themselves. For rulers [government] are not a cause
of fear for good behavior, but for evil. Do you want to
have no fear of authority? Do what is good, and you will
have praise from the same; for it is a minister of God to
you for good. But if you do what is evil, be afraid; for it
does not bear the sword [capital punishment] for nothing;
for it is a minister of God, an avenger [arbiter of justice]
who brings wrath upon the one who practices evil.
Wherefore it is necessary to be in subjection [to the au-
thority], not only because of wrath, but also for conscience' sake. For because of this you also pay taxes, for
rulers are servants of God, devoting themselves to this
very thing. Render to all what is due them: tax to whom
tax *is due*; custom to whom custom; fear to whom fear;
honor to whom honor. (Rom. 13:1–7)

God ordained that "rulers" should obey and defend the laws of divine establishment. Likewise, every inhabitant of a nation, whether believer or unbeliever, is exhorted to obey the authority of the ruler. Sig-
nificantly, Romans 13:1–7 was penned during the reign of the emperor
Nero, one of the most tyrannical and unjust regimes in the history of
the Roman Empire. The Scripture does not condone the practices of
any tyrant, but neither does oppressive governance negate the principle
of obedience to authority (Titus 2:15—3:1). Regardless of the character
of a ruler, his office represents the divinely delegated authority in that
nation. The office, if not the man, should always be respected.

IS REVOLUTION JUSTIFIED?

David exemplified obedience and deference to divinely appointed
authority even as he eluded the treachery of his sovereign, King Saul of
Israel. Possessed of a monstrous jealousy Saul sought the life of David,
his divinely anointed successor. David understood that Saul was re-
sponsible to God. In His own purpose and time God would remove
Saul and promote David. Thus, David refused to retaliate by taking
Saul's life or to allow his soldiers to assassinate Saul (1 Sam. 24:4, 6).
Assassination or revolution is never sanctioned by God.

Revolution is the deposing of the existing establishment or government and the destruction of divine institutions. The intent to overthrow one's own government either through plots and intrigue or by force of arms, including paramilitary activity, constitutes evil and is always contrary to divine will. Fomenting revolution leads to senseless mob violence and the lawless usurping of power. Whatever is gained in revolution could have been accomplished without revolution. The end never justifies the means. God swiftly punished Dathan and Abiram in their mutiny against Moses (Num. 16). Problems requiring divine establishment solutions can never be solved by violating divine establishment principles.

What about the American Revolutionary War of 1776? Was this rebellion against the governing authority? No! Ours was not a classic revolution in the manner of the French (1789) or Russian (1917) revolutions, but a war for independence. We did not overthrow the existing English government, abolish Parliament, eliminate the landowning aristocracy and replace them with street rabble and anarchists. We sought to perpetuate the divine institutions by establishing a republic that allowed the fullest expression of individual freedom.

NATIONAL CORRUPTION

There are always citizens in a nation who garner privilege without responsibility. They enjoy the benefits and protection of their country while giving their allegiance to a foreign government or a radical political or paramilitary group bent on insurrection. This destructive duplicity shatters the autonomy of a nation, as happened to Judea following the death and resurrection of Jesus Christ. Jewish political and religious leaders paid a bloody price for their hypocrisy. They exploited the benefits of Roman rule and patronage while simultaneously plotting against Caesar. As the social structure of Palestine disintegrated, the Roman procurator, Jewish leaders, Zealot rebels, and desperados of all sorts vied for power and plunder.[11]

When open war broke out in A.D. 66 thousands of Jews in Caesarea were massacred. By A.D. 68 Vespasian had isolated and surrounded Jerusalem. The siege concluded in A.D. 70 when Titus utterly destroyed the city, slaughtered and dispersed the populace, and brought

11. Bo Reicke, *The New Testament Era* (Philadelphia: Fortress Press, 1981), 210.

to an end any semblance of Jewish autonomy in Palestine until 1948.[12] The wages of their sedition were anarchy, bondage, and death. Freedom cannot survive such corruption in a society.

THE CLIENT NATION

At any period in history, somewhere in the world God ordains and maintains a client nation. This nation is God's specifically protected representative on earth, a repository for divine truth where the Gospel is freely communicated, doctrine is widely taught, and missionaries carry the Word of God to areas of positive volition throughout the world. The formation of such a nation begins with people who respond to the grace of God and become believers in Jesus Christ (Eph. 2:8–9). A nucleus of these Christians grows spiritually and forms a pivot of mature believers sufficient to sustain the nation and through which God furthers His plan for mankind. Israel was the client nation to God in the Old Testament era.

"'And you shall be to Me a kingdom of priests and a holy
nation [client nation].' These are the words that you shall
speak to the sons of Israel." (Ex. 19:6)

When both the Northern (721 B.C.) and Southern (586 B.C.) Kingdoms of Israel were destroyed under the fifth cycle of discipline, God's storehouse for doctrine resided with those faithful Jews dispersed throughout the Babylonian Empire and later the Persian Empire.[13] With the return of the Jews from captivity Israel again functioned as a client nation. Since the beginning of the Church Age on the day of Pentecost,

---

12. Thieme, *Anti-Semitism*, 76, 100; Josephus, "The Wars of the Jews," Book V, vi–xiii.

13. When Israel was saturated with apostasy, the client nation was warned by God through the increasing intensity of five cycles of discipline.

1. The first cycle: Loss of health, decline of agricultural prosperity, terror, fear, and death in combat, loss of personal freedoms due to negative volition toward Bible doctrine (Lev. 26:14–17).

2. The second cycle: Economic recession and depression, increased personal and individual discipline for continued negative volition in spite of the first warning (Lev. 26:18–20).

3. The third cycle: Violence and breakdown of law and order; severe restriction of travel and commerce (Lev. 26:21–22).

4. The fourth cycle: Military conquest and/or foreign occupation, scarcity of food (reduced to one-tenth the normal supply), separation of families (Lev. 26:23–26).

5. The fifth cycle: Destruction of the nation due to maximum rejection of biblical principles (Lev. 26:27–39).

A.D. 30, and the subsequent sack of Jerusalem in A.D. 70, only gentile nations are client nations. These nations have the additional responsibility to provide a haven for the Jews of the Diaspora. In the present age Jews who believe in Jesus Christ are part of the Church (Gal. 3:28).[14]

In the first century A.D. the Roman Empire became the setting for the incipient Church and the first gentile client nation. New Testament doctrine was written and widely circulated under SPQR, *Senatus Populesque Romanus*. Following the fall of Rome, subsequent client nations were the Ireland of Patrick in the fifth century A.D. and the Frankish Kingdom of Merovingians after A.D. 481; between the fifteenth and seventeenth centuries Switzerland in the time of Ulrich Zwingli and John Calvin; Scotland in the era of John Knox; France after the Edict of Nantes (1598); Sweden under Gustavus Adolphus; Brandenburg Prussia with the migration of the Huguenots from France after the revocation of the Edict of Nantes (1685). In the eighteenth and nineteenth centuries England manifested client nation status by providing the freedom for the communication of doctrine and supporting worldwide evangelism.

With the decline of the British Empire the United States now stands alone as the client nation. This country has been remarkably blessed by the Lord. Tragically, we have begun to degenerate from within. In the past few decades the spiritual life of many Christians has sunk to arrogant self-righteousness disguised as do-goodism and secular solutions to national and world problems. Our mission as a client nation is all but forgotten. The opportunity to glorify Jesus Christ through learning and applying Bible doctrine has been disregarded. Fewer and fewer believers are intent on spiritual growth and Gospel witness. More and more the insidious tactics of Christian activism—a zealous crusade for a moral cause—are replacing genuine Christian service. But the end never justifies the means.

In the angelic conflict Jesus Christ permits evil to run its course (Prov. 16:3–4). Yet the forward march of God's plan in history will inevitably crush any false system that man or Satan can devise. Although

---

14. Although Israel was set aside as a client nation in the Church Age, the Church does not become spiritual Israel nor are the unconditional covenants to the nation abrogated. God's promise to Abraham (Gen. 12:1–3; 13:15–16; 15:18; 22:15–18), to David (2 Sam. 7:8–16; Ps. 89:20–37), and to Israel in the New Covenant (Jer. 31:31–34) will be completely fulfilled to a regathered client nation of Israel in the Millennium.

God allows wicked nations to exist and may utilize them for His own purposes (Ps. 76:10a), He cannot permit a client nation to abuse its spiritual heritage. God may use evil nations to administer the fifth cycle of discipline to a client nation riddled with spiritual decay. When a client nation is removed, God raises a new one in its place.

The United States is not now and never has been a Christian nation.[15] We are a client nation to God, founded on divine establishment principles that ensure freedom for both Christian and non-Christian. In the past the foundation of doctrinally oriented, mature believers has been the source of divine blessing for the nation. Yet if believers today reject this spiritual legacy, we can expect to be destroyed, not only as a world power but as a free people and a client nation.

> My people are destroyed for lack of knowledge [of doctrine]. Because you have rejected knowledge, I also will reject you from being My priest [client nation]. Since you have forgotten the law of your God, I also will forget your children. (Hosea 4:6)

God is absolutely just. He will honor His Word resident in the souls of believers, even as the United States continues to decline. He will also preserve this client nation if a sufficient number of believers are consistently learning and applying His Word. Bible doctrine orients believers to the importance of the laws of divine establishment for the nation and to the priceless value of spiritual life in adversity and prosperity. Doctrinally oriented believers support law enforcement for protection against criminality and military preparedness for national security.

Gideon's "three hundred" offers a striking illustration of how doctrine in the soul of mature believers delivers a client nation (Judg. 7:5–7). God chose this unlikely leader from the least important tribe of Israel. When Gideon delivered an appeal for soldiers to fight against Midian, ten thousand men responded to the call (Judg. 7:3). However, knowing that not all these men had the mental attitude of courage to

---

15. The term "Christian nation" is a misnomer. Nations cannot be Christian; only individuals can become Christian. Based on their Judeo-Christian heritage our founding fathers provided for religious freedom in the Constitution of the United States. Although many of the inhabitants of this country profess Christianity, the laws of divine establishment, upon which the Constitution was based, were set up to insure the survival and blessing of Christians and non-Christians alike. Religious freedom depends upon the separation of church and state (Matt. 22:21; cf., Rom. 13:1–7).

fight, God whittled down the volunteers to three hundred who had for-titude. God honored this diminutive, doctrinally oriented force by using them to rout the Midianites and preserve the nation.

The survival and prosperity of the United States depend on such a pivot of mature believers.

> *Act* as free men, and do not use your freedom as a cover-ing for evil, but *use it* as bondslaves of God. (1 Pet. 2:16)

Only the grace of God can deliver this nation from its current predica-ment. We do not need overwhelming numbers; we just need enough mature believers for the Lord to use to accomplish His purpose.

CHURCH AND STATE

Although both church and state are ordained of God, they are al-ways to remain separate entities in the Church Age. God has separated the two in order to protect the world from the tyranny of religion. When church and state unite, freedom is destroyed as occurred in Spain during the Inquisition (1478–1834),[16] England under the Puritan Oliver Cromwell (1649–1658), France rescinding the Edict of Nantes under Louis XIV (1661–1715), and in some parts of South America today. Self-righteous Christian activists who gain power become vi-ciously intolerant of diverging theologies and tyrannical toward be-lievers and unbelievers. Believers are persecuted for the 'crime' of disagreement. Unbelievers may be forced into religious conversion de-nying them true volitional response to the Gospel.

The true Church, believers in Christ, should have influence on a national entity as invisible heroes but should never be identified as the state nor seek political control of the state.[17] When the principle of separation of church and state is disregarded, the results are disastrous to the citizens of that nation. Civil and religious freedoms disappear.

The influence of the Church is spiritual not activist. The presence of a pivot of mature believers obedient to Bible doctrine and the laws of divine establishment is the preserving influence on the national en-tity as "salt" (Matt. 5:13). Salt in the ancient world was a preservative.

---

16. Thieme, *Anti-Semitism*, 33–37.

17. The individual believer becomes an invisible hero by executing the plan of God and advancing to spiritual maturity. The mature believer has a powerful, unheralded, positive influence on other people, his nation, human history, and the angelic conflict.

The believer with Bible doctrine in the soul reflects the glory of God and becomes a witness to a lost and dying world (Matt. 5:14–16). Even a small pivot of mature believers can be the means of maintaining or restoring a client nation (Gen. 18:22–32).

In contrast the activist Christian loses his savor as the salt of the nation. Christian activism is built on the false philosophy that the end justifies the means, which ranges from civil disobedience to criminal violence. Believers who become activists seek to settle spiritual issues with political solutions. These arrogant, self-righteous Christians forget that spiritual issues belong to the believer alone. The spiritual life and values of the Church cannot be forced on the unbeliever or the believer. Only the separation of church and state gives both human and spiritual freedom allowing the optimum expression for human volition, which is the pivotal issue in the angelic conflict.

As a believer in Jesus Christ you have a tremendous responsibility in relation to the divine institutions. You have the latitude of individual choice—to make good or bad decisions; you have a duty to protect and provide for your family. Do you realize that you are also to protect other families? How? By understanding the principle of the separation of church and state and by fulfilling your responsibility to both (Matt. 22:21). You must grow spiritually and discharge the obligations of citizenship, including defending the nation as a soldier.

THE DEFENSE OF A NATION

The right of self-defense is the God-given prerogative of a national entity. The Book of Numbers authorizes the conscription and training of a military force for Israel. The call to arms, "whoever *was able to* go out to war," appears fourteen times in the first chapter. God brought the Jews of the Exodus out of Egypt for a purpose—to seize the land He promised them. Chapters 1—4, 10, 13, 26, and 31 delineate their mobilization plan: an order of battle (2:1–32); an alert system (10:7–8); an order of march (10:14–28); reconnaissance, intelligence gathering (13:1–21), and debriefing (13:26–33); a roll call of eligible males (26:1–51); a deployment for battle (31:3–6); and the division of plunder (31:11–54). Israel would be compelled to defend herself against a host of enemies. A military establishment and a battle plan were crucial. This same obligation of defense stands for any client nation.

The importance of spiritual life, national leadership, and military service to the freedom of a nation is further portrayed in the Book of Nehemiah. Nehemiah details God's military plan for defending the postexilic city of Jerusalem. As in Old Testament times, the spiritual life of believers, the divine establishment wisdom of those in authority, and a prepared and equipped military are essentials for preserving and defending our client nation.

Isagogical Background

Truly the Word of God is "alive and powerful," but translations are not always clear. Remember, the Bible is inspired only in the *original* languages of Hebrew and Aramaic in the Old Testament and Greek in the New Testament—*not* in English. Translations may not always articulate the true meaning of the original text. In addition, historical settings in the Bible include a variety of ancient cultures, all very different from our own, which affect word meanings.

When a study is made of any portion of the Word of God, several methods of inquiry are used. First, the student must orient to the historical time period in which the passage was written. Next, he must discern the categories of Bible doctrine covered and study the passages from this viewpoint. Finally, but of equal importance, is the analysis of the original language of the passage to accurately translate the text. Grammar, syntax, etymology, anachronisms, idiomatic phrases must be examined before a passage of Scripture can be correctly interpreted. This threefold biblical hermeneutic for studying God's Word is called "ICE":

Isagogics—the interpretation of Scripture within the framework of its historical setting or prophetical environment.

Categories—the hermeneutical principle of comparing Scripture with Scripture to determine the classification of doctrine.

Exegesis—a word-by-word, verse-by-verse, grammatical, syntactical, etymological, and contextual analysis of Scripture from the original languages of the Bible.

As we launch into a study of military preparedness in the Book of Nehemiah, the ICE approach is essential. Historical background and exegetical analysis must be covered so we might understand the dilemma the Jews faced on their return from Babylonian exile. Doctrine extracted from this study will orient us to the biblical view of the military in our society today.

HISTORICAL BACKGROUND

King David and his heir Solomon ruled the united twelve Hebrew tribes and expanded Israel's borders. After Solomon's death in 931 B.C. the client nation fragmented. Jeroboam led the ten northern tribes in rebellion (1 Kings 12:1–19), dividing the nation into the larger Northern Kingdom of Israel and the smaller Southern Kingdom of Judah that stretched from Jerusalem to the Negeb. The Northern Kingdom was destroyed and dispersed under the fifth cycle of discipline by the Assyrians in 721 B.C.

In 586 B.C. God used Nebuchadnezzar, king of Chaldea, as His instrument to bring chastisement on Jerusalem. Like the Northern Kingdom, Judah rejected divine directives and foundered in idolatry. Spiritual life within the nation ceased to exist. In the devastation that followed Nebuchadnezzar's conquest, the walls, palaces, and Solomon's temple in Jerusalem were leveled. The Jews lost not only all freedom and national autonomy but also their national sanctuary, God's dwelling place and the center of His worship. The Jews who survived the invasion were enslaved and forced to march nine hundred miles from Ramah to Babylon, a captivity which lasted seventy years.[18]

By 539 B.C. Babylon fell to the powerful empire of Persia.[19] In the next year (538 B.C.) Cyrus, king of Persia, decreed that fifty thousand Jews return to Palestine. These were the children or the grandchildren of the young men and women who suffered Nebuchadnezzar's wrath and endured the death march. Zerubbabel, the appointed governor of Judah, led the crucial expedition to rebuild the Temple, the focal point of spiritual life. Zerubbabel's temple was completed about 516 B.C. Ezra led a second expedition of Jews back from Babylonian exile around 458 B.C. (Ezra 7—10).

With the completion of the Temple, Jerusalem needed a defense system to protect the inhabitants and to preserve Temple worship. Nehemiah was God's chosen leader for the task of rebuilding the walls of Jerusalem. Like Daniel, who as an exile achieved high office in the

---

18. Thieme, *Daniel, Chapters One Through Six* (1996), 5–9.
19. Ibid., 121–55.

Chaldean and Persian Empires, Nehemiah was appointed at a young age by Artaxerxes (Longimanus), king of Persia, to the influential court position of cupbearer.[20] In this post of implicit trust and unimpeachable loyalty, Nehemiah's primary duty was to taste the wine of the monarch to insure that it was not poisoned. His lofty position required intimate and prolonged contact with the Persian royal family. Such close association undoubtedly allowed him to obtain a commission as governor of Judea and in 445 B.C. to return to Jerusalem with the authority to reconstruct the fortifications of the city. But the rebuilding of the defenses of Jerusalem did not go unopposed. Thus, the Book of Nehemiah emphasizes the importance of a strong military for preserving and prospering the spiritual, economic, and cultural life of a nation.

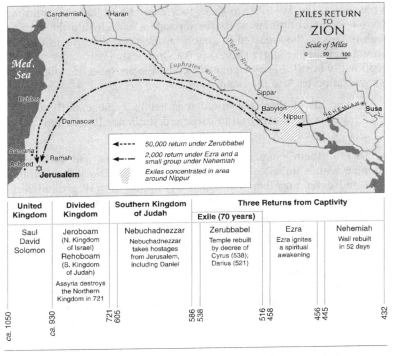

United Kingdom	Divided Kingdom	Southern Kingdom of Judah	Three Returns from Captivity		
			Exile (70 years)		
Saul David Solomon	Jeroboam (N. Kingdom of Israel) Rehoboam (S. Kingdom of Judah) Assyria destroys the Northern Kingdom in 721	Nebuchadnezzar Nebuchadnezzar takes hostages from Jerusalem, including Daniel	Zerubbabel Temple rebuilt by decree of Cyrus (538); Darius (521)	Ezra Ezra ignites a spiritual awakening	Nehemiah Wall rebuilt in 52 days
ca. 1050	ca. 930	721 605	586 538	516 458	456 445 432

---

20. During this period of the Persian monarchy the king's cupbearer exercised even more influence than the commander in chief. A. T. Olmstead, *History of the Persian Empire* (Chicago: The University of Chicago Press, 1970), 217.

Enemy Activity

> Now it came about when Sanballat, Tobiah, the Arabs,
> the Ammonites, and the Ashdodites heard that the repair
> of the walls of Jerusalem went on, *and* that the breaches
> began to be closed, they were very angry [חָרָה, *charah*].
> (Neh. 4:7)

Four neighboring tribes were threatened by the return of the Jews
and the reestablishment of a Jewish state: Sanballat was the leader of
the Samaritans, adversaries to the north; Tobiah led the Ammonites,
the eastern antagonists; Geshem (cf., Neh. 2:19) and the Arabs were
enemies to the south; and the Ashdodites, the surviving Philistines,
were foes to the west. When these four clans heard that the returning
Jews were erecting new walls for Jerusalem and closing the gaps in
their defenses, they reacted in anger. Of the several words in the Hebrew language for anger *charah* is the strongest. Their anger was ex-
ceptionally hostile. They were alarmed by the prospect of a mass Jewish migration back to the Land.

> And all of them conspired together to come *and* fight
> against Jerusalem and to cause a disturbance [confusion]
> in it. (Neh. 4:8)

"All of them" indicates the jealous neighbors had formed an
alliance with a united objective: to prevent the Jews from raising a
wall and defending their national sovereignty. A wall around Jerusalem would provide a haven for returning exiles. Without a bastion
for protection Jerusalem could be recaptured and destroyed anytime
her enemies determined to do so.

The conditions in Nehemiah's time bear a striking similarity to the
situation in the Middle East in the first years of the twenty-first century. Since the founding of the new Jewish state in 1948, hundreds of
thousands of Jews have migrated to Israel. Surrounding Arab states
have resisted this reemergence of Jews in the Land. Consequently, the
Jews have been forced to fight or be driven into the sea. Israel's freedom and autonomy are still contingent upon the strength and readiness
of her military.[21]

---

21. Thieme, *Anti-Semitism*, xiv–2.

Similarly, the United States is not without enemies. Yet we have stripped our military to bare bones. Our armed services are woefully inadequate for effectively defending our vital interests abroad. Nehemiah 4:8 encourages us to revitalize and maintain the military. We should consider Israel's continuing struggle for survival and heed the warnings of Nehemiah. We should realize that our enemies will always oppose the rebuilding of our martial capabilities even as the four tribes vigorously opposed the rebuilding of Jerusalem's wall.

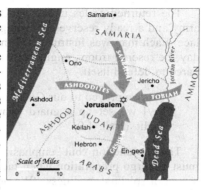

"All of them conspired together to come" indicates the hostile approach of the four armies to Jerusalem. Their objective: Make war against the city from all sides. These diverse groups joined forces in a plot to destroy Jerusalem. "To cause a disturbance," תּוֹעָה (*to'ah*), actually denotes creating "confusion" to facilitate the purpose of the alliance. Clearly, these armies were bent on exploitation, tyranny, and enslavement.

The National Response

When the exiled Jews returned to the Land, they accomplished two tasks: First, they restored the function of the Temple, revitalizing their spiritual life as the highest priority; second, they provided for national defense by rebuilding the walls of Jerusalem and their military establishment. Mandatory military training was instituted. They were following the time-honored tradition mandated by the Mosaic Law.

> And Moses spoke to the people, saying, "Arm men from among you for the war [learn the use of arms and train for warfare], that they may go against Midian, to execute the LORD'S vengeance on Midian. A thousand from each tribe of all the tribes of Israel you shall send to the war." So there were furnished from the thousands of Israel, a thousand from each tribe, twelve thousand armed [trained] for war. (Num. 31:3–5)

The returned exiles under Nehemiah maintained a small, regular army and a ready reserve consisting of the entire eligible male populace. Each man was instructed in the use of a weapon. On any given day the reserve troops might be soldiers or civilians. Judah was prepared to defend itself.

> But we prayed to our God, and because of them [the enemy] we set up a guard [watch] against them day and night. (Neh. 4:9)

The conjunction "but" emphasizes the two areas in which a nation must undergo preparation when facing an antagonist. Notice first the aspect of spiritual readiness. "We prayed (פָּלַל, *palal*) to our God" literally means, "But from our own free will, we offered intercessory prayer to our God." They prefaced their operational preparations with a petition to the Lord.

The second priority of a nation is military readiness. "A guard against them day and night," מִשְׁמָר עֲלֵיהֶם יוֹמָם וָלַיְלָה (*mishmar 'aleyhem yomam valaylah*), is a phrase encapsulating four critical spheres of grand strategy for national defense:[22]

1. The ability to mobilize a military force to meet an invading army;
2. Constant readiness and training;
3. A sagacious and establishment-oriented civilian administration;
4. A united civilian populace that supports a common national objective.

With foresight the Jewish leaders had organized for any contingency and were able to counter the threat of the aggressively approaching armies. Since they had already established a superb military organization that could be rapidly mobilized, the troops now were placed on maximum alert.

Their determination to defend Jerusalem reveals something about the Jew of ancient Israel. Like his counterpart in the modern state of Israel, he was a formidable soldier, a ferocious fighter who exhibited courage, resourcefulness, and mental toughness in the face of aggression.

---

22. Grand strategy is the science and art of employing the political, economic, psychological, and military forces of a nation to afford maximum support of adopted policies in peace and war.

In the phrase "set up a guard against them," the verb עָמַד (*'amad*) means "to be caused to be stabilized, to take one's stand" and the noun *mishmar* means "a guard" or "a watch." These Jews were vigilant and ready for action. While the apostate Jews in the days of Jeremiah neglected and rejected their military, the steadfast Jews under Nehemiah had a fully staffed, well-trained military establishment. Clearly the returned exiles had learned from their past mistakes.

Internal Opposition

Thus in Judah it was said,
"The strength of the burden bearers is failing,
Yet there is much rubbish;
And we ourselves are unable
To rebuild the wall." (Neh. 4:10)

Some of the Jews complained that they could not reconstruct the defensive wall around the city as long as full mobilization was in effect. When Nehemiah called up the reserves, that left only the "burden bearers," an exhausted crew of rock carriers, still clearing the "rubbish." The wall had been devastated in Nebuchadnezzar's siege and was still in deplorable condition, useless for protecting the inhabitants. So much rubble remained that the builders could not maneuver to begin reconstruction of the ramparts. Faced with an impending attack and too little time to rebuild, Nehemiah decided to develop defensive tactics with a fully mustered legion and to trust in the Lord for deliverance.[23]

While verse 10 reveals the internal discord among the returned exiles, verse 11 describes the plotting of the enemy from without.

And our enemies said, "They [the Jews] will not know or see [the plot] until we [invaders] come among them, kill them, and put a stop to the work." (Neh. 4:11)

The armies of the Samaritans, the Arabs, the Philistines, and the Ammonites finalized their strategy for a surprise attack and converged on Jerusalem. Unbeknown to these conspirators the element of surprise would have no effect. The Jewish army, well trained and on full alert, was prepared.

---

23. Tactics constitute the methods used to employ troops in combat.

The four aggressors understood the difficulty of attacking a prepared military defense. They opted for the shock of surprise, to catch
the defenders unawares. Their immediate objective was to kill the exiles already in Jerusalem. Their long-range objective was to discour-
age any new contingent of returning Jewish refugees from completing
the defensive bulwark of Jerusalem's massive walls.

> And it came about when the Jews who lived near them
> [the invaders] came and told us ten times, "They will
> come up against us from every place where you may
> turn." (Neh. 4:12).

Even though Nehemiah inaugurated mandatory military training,
even though the army was prepared for every exigency, even though
the general populace would fight to avoid enslavement and annihilation, there were still some cowards who wanted to surrender. Jews
from outlying areas had reconnoitered the approaching armies and
could see no escape. Terrified over the possibility of attack, they
flocked to the city frantically repeating a warning to Nehemiah, "Our
enemies are coming from every direction—we are trapped!" Knowing
such hysteria could spread to the troops and the public at large, Nehemiah took decisive action.

Military Preparation

> Then I stationed *men* in the lowest parts of the space be-
> hind the wall, the exposed places, and I stationed the peo-
> ple in families [מִשְׁפָּחָה, *mishpachah*] with their swords,
> spears, and bows. (Neh. 4:13)

After estimating the situation Nehemiah issued an operations order.
He arrayed the troops in a defensive posture to meet the enemy strategy. Nehemiah was not only a student of the Word of God, but also of
military science and human nature. He used the terrain and the available forces to best advantage. Lacking a completed wall around the
city, he set up a defensive perimeter, concentrating troops at the gaps
in the fortifications to act as a holding force.

How could such a sparse first line of defense hold in the face of a
numerically superior force? Nehemiah literally stationed his troops in
their *mishpachah*, "clans." Each combat unit consisted of extended

family members. In close proximity to each unit were wives, children, and other noncombatant relatives. Thus the soldiers were placed in naturally cohesive groups and furnished with a constant reminder of the dire consequences that defeat would bring to their loved ones. This family immediacy would give the warriors added incentive to fight on to victory. What a brilliant and innovative command decision! Nehemiah exhibited exceptional moral courage, an essential attribute for any military leader.

Then, he formulated a strategy to place these "*men in the lowest parts*" to hide the main body of his troops from the enemy. In so doing, regardless of which enemy army attacked first, Nehemiah could call on his hidden reserve forces to meet the most prominent threat. Nehemiah had thus provided a defensive perimeter around the city and a mobile reserve to maneuver on interior lines.[24] The advantage of fighting on interior lines is the ability to concentrate all available combat power against the most immediate danger. A smaller force can preserve the initiative against a larger force. Clearly Nehemiah understood strategy and tactics.

Hidden from sight on the low ground, Nehemiah set up his mobile reserve, his instant reaction force. Their position shielded them from the prying eyes of the enemy. The hostile forces theoretically would observe only the weak perimeter and then proceed recklessly, confident of easy victory. At just the right moment, Nehemiah would move the reaction force and strike the attacking enemy on the flank. Thus, the enemy would face a tenacious holding force and a second aggressive force, attacking from a different angle. Here is the advantage of fighting on interior lines. After the enemy is defeated in one quadrant, the reaction force can move quickly to a different section of the perimeter and respond to a threat from a new direction.

Notice again the last phrase of verse 13, "with their swords, spears, and bows." The Jews had weapons and they knew how to use them. They had the means and the will to protect their country and their loved ones. Disarmament is never an option for a people desiring freedom.

---

24. The strategy of interior lines means striking outwards from a central pivot against one of the forces on the circumference, and utilizing the shorter distance to travel to concentrate against one of the enemy forces before it can be supported by the others. See B.H. Liddell Hart, *Strategy* (New York: Praeger Publishers, 1975), 108.

From Nehemiah's example an application can be made to the United States of America. From time to time the freedom of this country depends on general officers who accurately understand and skillfully employ the military science of strategy and tactics. Only after years of intense training and study in technical military subjects is a commander capable of deftly and effectively maneuvering troops. Such proficiency comes only through constant practice and preparation. Yet this country has discouraged gifted men from dedicating their lives to the study of military science. Those who have chosen to follow the noble profession of arms receive little honor from those they serve. Often they are hated and ridiculed by their countrymen. What a tragedy! No nation can survive in time of war without such courageous and competent soldiers.

Civilian Preparation

When I [Nehemiah] saw *their fear*, I rose and spoke to the nobles, the officials, and the rest of the people: "Do not be afraid of them; remember the Lord who is great and awesome, and fight for your brothers, your sons, your daughters, your wives, and your houses." (Neh. 4:14).

Who was Nehemiah addressing? The aristocracy, the bureaucracy, and all the rest of the citizens. Nehemiah knew the danger of fear spreading among the military and civilian leadership and the populace in general. Fear would not only cause the leadership to overreact and issue orders contradictory to Nehemiah's, but would also paralyze the civilians. Nehemiah did not need the leadership's interference in his strategic and tactical decisions; he needed them to prepare themselves "and the rest of the people" for the coming battle. So Nehemiah encouraged all of them to think divine viewpoint.

Nehemiah reminded all the citizens why they should not panic. Fear on the home front can be just as devastating to the war effort as fear in the foxhole. Such fear can subvert national morale and sabotage a people's determination to defend freedom. He urged all of them to focus on Bible doctrine. Nehemiah's rallying cry was "Do not be afraid of them; remember the Lord!" In effect he was saying to them, "You have doctrine, now use it!"

When I am afraid,
I will put my trust in Thee. (Ps. 56:3)

The LORD is for me; I will not fear;
What can man do to me? (Ps. 118:6)

"Do not fear, for I am with you;
Do not anxiously look about you, for I am your God.
I will strengthen you, surely I will help you,
Surely I will uphold you with My righteous right hand."
   (Isa. 41:10)

Nehemiah did not divulge his strategy of fighting on interior lines, the tactic of envelopment, or his ingenious troop dispositions. Security of the operation was paramount. He could not risk the possibility of his carefully laid plans falling into enemy hands through a slip of the tongue.

Nehemiah had no time for situation briefings or a long sermon. All his concentration was on the coming conflict. Success in any endeavor in life requires the concentration to pay attention to detail while staying focused on the objective. However, Nehemiah remained a brief moment to remind them that the Lord is "great and awesome"; their God was a mighty warrior, "the Lord of hosts," the ultimate Commander in Chief. With the Mighty Warrior in control what did Israel have to fear from her enemies? Nehemiah exhorted them to employ the faith-rest drill[25] so they could handle their fear and invoke the battle cry of King David:

"The battle is the LORD'S and He will give you [the enemy] into our hands." (1 Sam. 17:47b)

'Do not fear or be dismayed because of this great multitude, for the battle is not yours but God's.' (2 Chron. 20:15b)

God uses warfare to judge nations which have become depraved. At various times in the course of Israel's history the Lord of hosts had given the command "utterly destroy them [the enemy]!" to keep

---

25. The faith-rest drill is the technique for claiming scriptural promises and applying them to the circumstances of life. See Thieme, *Christian, at Ease!* (1993), 15–18; *The Faith-Rest Life* (1999); *Armageddon* (2002), 28; see below "Victory over Fear—The Ten Problem-Solving Devices," 69.

corruption from spreading or to preserve His people (Deut. 7:2, 16; 20:16–17; Josh. 11:20–21). In 1 Chronicles 5 the Jews were fighting the Hagrites, descendants of Hagar, the Egyptian servant of Sarah and Abraham (Gen. 16:1–10). God condoned this war as judgment upon Canaanite apostasy.

> And they made war against the Hagrites, Jetur, Naphish, and Nodab. And they were helped against them, and the Hagrites and all who *were* with them [their allies] were given into their hand; for they [the Jews] cried out to God in the battle, and He was entreated for them [their cause was just], because they trusted [faith-rest] in Him. (1 Chron. 5:19–20)

> For many fell slain, because the war *was* of God. (1 Chron. 5:22a)

This is the divine perspective of warfare: Victory demands that the enemy be rendered *hors de combat*. Wars should be fought to win and winning means slaying the enemy.

Nehemiah 4:14 closes with the command, "Fight for your brothers, your sons, your daughters, your wives, and your houses." This mandate reminds the warriors why they fight:

"For your brothers"—fight to defend your fellow citizens, the national entity, divine institution number four;

"Your sons, your daughters"—fight to defend and protect children and family, divine institution number three;

"Your wives"—fight to protect your right woman, divine institution number two;

"Your houses"—fight to defend privacy, property, and freedom, divine institution number one.

Warfare is necessary as the guardian of the four divine institutions. Nehemiah not only calmed the fears of all the citizenry by encouraging them to "remember the Lord," but he motivated the military by reminding them of the common cause for which they would confront the enemy—the freedom of the nation. He personalizes this command by saying, "Fight for the survival and well-being of your families."

If you are a soldier, memorize the last phrase of verse 14. When you find yourself in combat on a foreign shore thousands of miles from

home, remember you are fighting for your loved ones. No matter where
the fray, or who the enemy, you are waging war for hearth and home.

Military Preparation Prevents Wars

> And it happened when our enemies heard that it [the sur-
> prise attack] was known to us, and that God had frus-
> trated their plan, then all of us returned to the wall, each
> one to his work. (Neh. 4:15)

Having "frustrated" the machinations of the four enemies, the crisis
passed without bloodshed. Why? The Jews were prepared for
war—'peace through strength!' God honored Nehemiah's compliance
with the divine defense plan. The Jews were ready and willing to defend their freedom without reservation. Thus, the four aggressor nations were deterred and retired without attempting an assault. The
epitome of military preparedness is to deter the enemy without a fight.

How different is the story of the United States. After World War I
the military capacity of our country was drastically reduced by a de-
luded Congress. Our representatives mistakenly believed we had just
won 'the war to end all wars.' Such is never the case. Why did the
Japanese attack Pearl Harbor? They saw an easy target! The Japanese
took advantage of our appalling weakness. They planned to crush our
under strength army and navy in the Pacific with one blow, leaving us
helpless to resist. Had our military been adequately prepared for aggression, the surprise attack on Pearl Harbor might have remained
only a scenario of Admiral Yamamoto and the Japanese Imperial staff
rather than the reality of 7 December 1941.

By the end of World War II our military power reached its zenith.
But rather than intelligent demobilization to maintain a semblance of the
most effective fighting force in the history of our nation, we drastically
reduced the army, mothballed the fleet, and gave up important strategic
advantages. Through irresponsible reduction of forces we were once
again left vulnerable. How quickly we forgot the price of freedom.

Within five years of World War II we were mired in the Korean
War for which we were shockingly ill-prepared in personnel and
equipment. Ten years later we committed troops to combat in Vietnam, untrained in guerrilla warfare and with no intelligible objective.
The civilian population—Americans enjoying the privileges of

freedom—abandoned our soldiers fighting on that distant, jungle battlefield. We forfeited morale, men, materiel, prestige, and self-respect. Are we destined to repeat continually the painful lesson taught by our lack of military preparedness? The old axiom seems to apply: We learn from history that we learn nothing from history.

In contrast the Jews applied divine viewpoint and learned the lesson of history. Nehemiah's established war plan, speedy mobilization, brilliant tactical deployment of troops, and the support of the civilian population disheartened the four invading armies. The price of attacking a primed defense was too high. When oppressors identify a tough opponent, their resolve falters.

Since Nehemiah and his compatriots understood divine viewpoint, especially the doctrine of the total depravity of man, they had no illusions about the evil intent of the invaders. Totalitarian nations harbor sinister intentions. Spiritual and military training are necessary to prevent tyranny from prevailing. The Jews, both spiritually and militarily prepared, could now prudently demobilize the reserves and finish reconstructing the walls—an engineering feat they accomplished in a remarkable fifty-two days (Neh. 6:15).

Intelligent Demobilization

And it came about from that day on, that half of my servants carried on the work while half of them held the spears, the shields, the bows, and the breastplates; and the captains *were* behind the whole house of Judah. (Neh. 4:16)

The reserves were demobilized and "carried on the work" of raising the wall. The rock carriers welcomed the help they had been begging for while the regular army maintained constant readiness. The regulars, still mobilized, carried their weapons. This is the shrewd way to demobilize. The Jews realized their enemies could return without warning. They were not only equipped militarily for such a contingency, but also were improving their defensive capability by rebuilding the wall. They had learned the cost of maintaining freedom and national autonomy. It cannot be negotiated with an implacable enemy. Freedom is the product of constant vigilance, military might, and in the final analysis, the grace of God.

Whereas Judah had four unrelenting foes, the United States has countless antagonists and few real allies. Absurd military reductions have made our country dangerously vulnerable. We cannot maintain freedom from a position of weakness—either military or spiritual weakness. We must follow Judah's example and pay the price for freedom by supporting an extensive and proficient military.

Nehemiah 4:16 concludes by emphasizing the importance of leadership during Judah's demobilization. The rulers "behind the whole house of Judah" were leaders who understood the necessity of a well-trained military supported by the home front. They organized the people both to work and to fight.

The rebuilding of the United States armed forces in the 1980s brought our long-standing antagonist, the Soviet Union, to dissolution without a shooting war. Our defense priority was an astute application of the concept of freedom and peace through strength. Where is that kind of leadership in the United States today? In the past, both the executive and legislative branches of government had denigrated and denuded the military. As a result our national defense was impaired.

The next two verses continue to recount the Jewish demobilization.

> Those [the demobilized troops] who were rebuilding the wall and those who carried burdens [the rock carriers] took *their* load with one hand doing the work and the other holding a weapon. (Neh. 4:17)

> As for the builders, each *wore* his sword girded at his side as he built, while the trumpeter *stood* near me. (Neh. 4:18)

Why were the builders wearing swords? Because these citizen-soldiers—professional construction workers and expert men-at-arms—were essential to the Jewish defense force. While the men worked on the wall, they kept their weapons instantly available. Nehemiah did not intend for the enemy to return and surprise the Jews before they could complete the fortifications around Jerusalem. The military was so integral to the survival of freedom that participation was a duty for every able-bodied man. The demobilized reserves carried their weapons to work and were ready to use them at a moment's notice. They were true "minutemen." Their call to arms was only a trumpet sound away. They were spiritually, militarily, and mentally prepared. Freedom so zealously guarded is freedom preserved.

THE DIVINE VIEWPOINT OF THE MILITARY

The following biblical tenets will illuminate your thinking concerning the purpose and necessity of the military. God authorizes a military so the human race can survive war and guard freedom, just as He authorizes the "sword" of state (Rom. 13:4) so the human race can survive crime and live in freedom.

Freedom must be maintained.
The military maintains freedom.
Therefore, the military must be maintained.

Protection of the Nation

Enemies may appear from within or from without the nation. Scripture supports the right of law-abiding citizens to defend themselves against evil and crime and a nation to defend against hostile attack. Violence of evildoers is restrained only by the stronger violence of the righteous. God could not be called good if "He were to turn the world over to the horrors of unbridled cruelty perpetrated by violent and bloody criminals or the unchecked aggression of invading armies."[26]

In the operation of the military in combat the enemy must be destroyed to protect freedom. The same is true of the enemy within: The violent criminal must be removed from society—therefore, the necessity of imprisonment and capital punishment. The military destroys external enemies; the judicial system executes internal enemies. Thus, peace and the survival of a nation are ensured.

INTERIOR PROTECTION

God ordained government to be the authority within a national entity. As the guardian of liberty, a regime, whatever its form of governance (parliamentary, monarchy, republic, etc.), must protect the inherent right of its citizens to life, privacy, property, and freedom to succeed or fail according to their own ability and volition. The national entity must also ensure the right of the individual to religious freedom—the opportunity

---

26. Gleason L. Archer, *Encyclopedia of Bible Difficulties* (Grand Rapids: Zondervan Publishing House, 1982), 219.

to accept or reject Jesus Christ as Savior (Acts 17:26–28) and grow in the spiritual life (2 Pet. 3:18).

Civil liberty is maintained through an objective judicial system that is respected by a majority of citizens. The authority of the policeman on the corner and the judge on the bench protect freedom within a nation. The police officer detects and deters criminal activity, apprehends offenders, and keeps public order. Judges as leaders or authorities in the state are "ministers of God" (Rom. 13:4) divinely ordained to adjudicate and to punish. A system for establishing evidence in trials, administering strict punitive measures for the guilty (Eccl. 8:11), and obtaining the immediate release of the innocent characterizes equitable jurisprudence. The entire internal security of a people depends on just and skillful administration of law, which protects the innocent and punishes the guilty.

EXTERIOR PROTECTION

A nation that adheres to the laws of divine establishment is a righteous power that provides a bulwark against any encroaching forces of tyranny and evil. An honorable military defends national sovereignty. Obviously, military invasion for personal or political aggrandizement, such as the Nazis in World War II or the later communist aggressions, is not justified. Battlefield victories won by virtuous nations forced to employ *justified* violence have preserved freedom throughout history.

Does a nation protect its sovereignty and freedom when it fights an enemy on foreign soil? The biblical answer is delineated in Numbers 32. Two of the tribes of Israel, Reuben and Gad, requested their parcel of promised land on the east side of the Jordan River (v. 5). The rest of the nation's land was to be on the west side of the river. Moses was incensed that Reuben and Gad wanted to desert their fellow Israelites about to begin the battle for dominion west of the river (v. 6). Reuben and Gad corrected their mistake in a response to Moses.

> And the sons of Gad and the sons of Reuben answered, saying, "As the LORD has said to your servants, so we will do. We ourselves will cross over armed in the presence of the LORD into the land of Canaan, and the possession of our inheritance *shall remain* with us across [east of] the Jordan." (Num. 32:31–32)

Reuben and Gad were saying in effect, "We are fighting for our land by crossing the river and fighting on the other side." These two tribes realized that their freedom and autonomy depended upon defeating the common enemy of the entire nation, even though that foe was beyond the borders of their own territory. They would not wait for the enemy to attack their domain but would strike first to spare their families and property from the devastation of war.

When Charles Martel organized a group of warriors and drove the followers of Mohammed back behind the Pyrenees Mountains at the battle of Tours, Europe was saved from centuries of Islamic rule (A.D. 732). Had it not been for a few Polish, Austrian, Prussian, Hungarian, and Greek knights who had the courage to oppose Genghis Khan and his invading Mongol armies, Western Europe would have been subjected to centuries of barbaric Tatar domination.[27] With overwhelming power and might the United States of America annihilated the tyranny of Japan and Germany in World War II. Decisive defeat of an enemy is the only way to assure autonomy. Such violence is justified to deter evil aggression and perpetuate freedom.

PEACE THROUGH A PREPARED MILITARY

To insure peace a nation must be prepared for war. Military weakness invites attack by belligerent, aggressive nations. Military superiority deters aggression. Only those living in a fool's paradise support shirking military service, antiwar demonstrations, and disarmament.

Understandably, man desires peace, and freedom is optimized during times of tranquillity, but the manner of achieving and maintaining peace has been the subject of endless controversy throughout history. Unrealistic utopians advocate world peace through capitulation, assuming

---

27. The fearsome name "Tatar" given to the Mongol hordes was derived and altered from the Greek word Τάρταρος (*Tartaros*) or the Latin "Tartarus," meaning "a place of torment," reflecting their reputation as more devils than human. The rapacious savagery of Genghis Khan and subsequent Mongol armies of the thirteenth century turned Asian civilization into a wasteland. Wherever the Tatars went devastation and slaughter marked their path. Tatar military success "seemed to have been due to their excellent organization: unified command, general staff, clever intelligence service, and deceptive battle tactics." Crane Brinton, John B. Christopher, and Robert Lee Wolff, eds., *A History of Civilization* (Englewood Cliffs, New Jersey: Prentice-Hall, Inc., 1967), 1:368.

harmony can be created among nations through good will.[28] These 'doves,' apostles of appeasement, foster warfare. They beg and cry for peace "but there is no peace" (Jer. 6:14b; Ezek. 13:10a). Safety is never attained by 'petting the cobra' or peacefully coexisting with the tiger. Those who try end up peacefully dead. When a nation caters to confused idealists dreaming of a better world or hoping to bring in the Millennium through disarmament and pacifism, that nation is being led to the slaughter.

> He has put forth his hands against those who were at
>   peace with him;
> He has violated his covenant.
> His speech was smoother than butter,
> But his heart was war;
> His words were softer than oil [deceptive],
> Yet they were drawn swords. (Ps. 55:20–21)

Throughout history deceptive words have been uttered to mask "drawn swords." Wicked nations proclaim peace when their true intent is to wage war and subjugate other nations (Ezek. 13:10–16). These deceivers extend an olive branch in one hand while concealing a sword in the other. The plight of a people desiring peace who are plagued by a belligerent enemy is described by the psalmist.

> Too long has my soul had its dwelling
> With those who hate peace.
> I am *for* peace, but when I speak,
> They are for war. (Ps. 120:6–7)

Nations plead for peace, negotiate treaties to guarantee peace, make compromises and concessions for peace, only to be bitterly disappointed when the peace is violated and freedom threatened. What is the response to the machinations of deceitful nations?

Historically, a balance of power against aggressive nations has been the most effective insurance for an interval of peace. The only way to avoid war is to be adequately equipped and trained for war. In

---

28. Such fanciful idealism is epitomized by William Godwin (1756–1836), the English writer and philosopher, who declared that "the buildup of military power and forging of military alliances, or balance-of-power policies, were likely to lead to war." See Thomas Sowell, *A Conflict of Visions* (New York: William Morrow and Company, Inc., 1987), 145.

any generation the capability for righteous violence is essential for the preservation of national freedom. Only a prepared national military can deter enemy aggression.[29]

The Inevitability of War

Despite man's efforts for peace, warfare will continue until the Millennium (Matt. 24:6; Mark 13:7; Luke 21:9). Never in human history has there been a time when warfare has not been raging in some corner of the globe. In the period from 1990 through 1995 fifty-three separate major armed conflicts were recorded.[30] The sin nature, mankind's volition, and the cunning stratagems of Satan in the angelic conflict are the root causes. After the Rapture of the Church,[31] during the seven years of the Tribulation conflicts will become even more brutal (Rev. 6—19). Only at His second advent when the Lord Jesus Christ victoriously concludes the Armageddon campaign will warfare cease.[32] Satan and all fallen angels will be removed from the earth (Rev. 20:1–3). Then, with Jesus Christ on the throne of the millennial kingdom, hostilities will no longer threaten the peace of nations (Isa. 11:6–9; Micah 4:1–3).

---

29. The concept of deterrence as applied since World War II is described by Lt. Gen. Franz Uhle-Wettler: "None of the causes which have brought about innumerable wars has been eliminated. The causes were all there, but peace has been preserved because both sides feared the consequences of the first shot. This has been interpreted as indicating that the causes of war can indeed be controlled, and that they can best be controlled through widespread fear of war (the concept of deterrence)." *Brassey's Encyclopedia of Military History and Biography*, 1994 ed., s.v. "War," by Franz Uhle-Wettler.

30. Uppsala University, Department of Peace and Conflict Research, Uppsala, Sweden. This organization categorizes a major armed conflict as any warfare that has accumulated greater than one thousand deaths since the beginning of the clash.

31. The Rapture, or ἐξανάστασις (exanastasis), "exit resurrection," is the resurrection of all living and dead Church Age believers from the earth to meet the Lord in the air and become the Bride of Christ (1 Thess. 4:14–17). The Rapture takes place at the end of the Church Age immediately before the Tribulation. God's sovereign decision determines the time of the Rapture; no man knows the day or hour (Matt. 24:42; 25:13; Mark 13:32).

32. Armageddon (Rev. 16:12–16) is the last battle of the last campaign of the last war of history that takes place on the plain of Esdraelon near the city of Megiddo in which the forces of the returned Lord Jesus Christ defeat the forces of gentile world powers bent on annihilating Israel (Rev. 19:11–21). Thieme, *Armageddon*, 8.

And He will judge between the nations,
And will render decisions for many peoples;
And they will hammer their swords into plowshares, and
    their spears into pruning hooks.
Nation will not lift up sword against nation,
And never again will they learn war. (Isa. 2:4)

Until Christ returns in glory warfare is inevitable (Eccl. 3:8) and under certain circumstances necessary for maintaining national sovereignty and preserving freedom.

THE MILITARY IMAGE OF JESUS CHRIST

During the struggle to attain and perpetuate Jewish freedom after the Exodus, the preincarnate Jesus Christ reserved the title the "Lord of hosts," Lord of the armies of Israel (2 Kings 19:31a). In the Book of Joshua He is called "Captain of the Lord's host." Jesus Christ was the Commander in Chief; Joshua was the chief of staff (Josh. 5:13—6:2). Joshua received a mandate from the Lord to destroy certain enemies (Josh. 11:6; cf., Deut. 20:15–18) so Israel might be preserved. This mandate, directed toward the destruction of a society saturated in degeneracy, included the divinely authorized killing of men, women, and children. Only then could the people of Israel disentangle themselves from the pervasive and contagious evil of a depraved society.

No leader today carries divine authority to kill civilian men, women, and children. However, in the course of all warfare noncombatants regrettably become casualties. Although such losses are to be avoided, God still sanctions the destruction of the enemy in battle to attain victory and maintain freedom. At the word of the Lord Jesus Christ, the Assyrian army of 185,000 infantrymen was struck down in one night (Isa. 37:36). At the close of the Tribulation, Jesus Christ will use righteous violence to decimate the military powers invading the Middle East (Zech. 14:3). The blood will run as high as the horses' bridles (Rev. 14:20).

And from His mouth comes a sharp sword, so that with it He may smite the nations [at Armageddon]; and He will rule them with a rod of iron; and He treads the wine press of the fierce wrath of God, the Almighty. And on His robe and on His thigh He has a name written, "KING OF KINGS, AND LORD OF LORDS [Jesus Christ]." (Rev. 19:15–16)

Today pacifist believers would probably censure the Lord Jesus Christ if they understood the full impact of this passage. They envision Him as the meek and mild Jesus who spoke of turning the other cheek in the Sermon on the Mount (Matt. 5:39). In reality He is the one who "smites the nations." The Sermon on the Mount relates to His personal peaceful reign over the earth that will not be initiated until the Millennium.

The "sharp sword" of verse 15 is the most formidable weapon of all time. With the words "from His mouth" our Lord slays the armies at Armageddon. The imagery of "the wine press" signifies the massive slaughter that terminates the Armageddon campaign. Christ Himself demonstrates how to win a war: Kill the enemy. Jesus Christ does not return at the Second Advent to negotiate a peace settlement; He returns to destroy the enemy. After their annihilation warfare will cease; freedom and peace will reign for a thousand years.

Nations That Lose Wars Lose Freedom

National autonomy and well-being inevitably depend on a superior army. A nation perpetuates freedom when its military succeeds but risks enslavement when its military fails. A strong military establishes a buffer against conflict. A nation cannot survive the destruction of its armed forces.

Military defeat and enslavement are part of the consequences of the demise of every client nation under the fifth cycle of discipline (Lev. 26:27–39). Before this catastrophic divine judgment descends upon a nation every echelon of spiritual and national life, including the military establishment, degenerates. Both the Northern Kingdom of Israel (721 B.C.) and the Southern Kingdom of Judah (586 B.C.), destitute of spiritual virtue and values, followed this road to ruin.

Nonclient nations that disdain the laws of divine establishment also suffer devastating divine judgment. The Assyrians gradually deteriorated over thirty years before their capital, Nineveh, fell in 612 B.C. Chaldea, in the process of decay since the death of Nebuchadnezzar in 562 B.C., was easily subdued by the Persians in 539 B.C. Thus, when any nation's armed forces are neglected, demoralized, and unprepared to wage war, that nation is in grave danger of losing a war and forfeiting the autonomy and freedom of its people.

Athens and Carthage reflect the tragedy of freedom lost on the battlefield. After a generation of conflict besieged and starving Athenians surrendered to a cruel and deceitful Sparta in 404 B.C., ending the Peloponnesian War. Athens was shorn of its empire and the sun set over the glory of Greece. Carthage was utterly destroyed in the Third Punic War (149–146 B.C.): Every building was burned to the ground, the site sown with salt to render farming futile, and all remaining territories were confiscated by Rome.[33]

The wars of Napoleon, from the Italian campaign to the battle at Austerlitz (1795–1805), depict the value of preparedness. The *Grande Armee* was the most formidable fighting force in Europe. With the borders of France secure from invasion the cowed nations on the continent lost all desire to challenge French ascendancy. These early campaigns of the Napoleonic era demonstrate the principle that the superior army obtains and maintains freedom and autonomy for its nation.

The German conquest of Norway in World War II offers another illustration. Vidkun Quisling, whose infamous name became synonymous with traitor, undermined the military's effectiveness and will to fight. The Nazis needed only a few battalions to subjugate all Norway. Consequently, the country suffered the horrors of Nazi occupation for the rest of the war.

Throughout the history of the United States our army has traditionally been ill-equipped to wage war. Only after we experienced appalling casualties did our national spirit arise to mobilize a magnificent army to meet an enemy on two fronts in World War II. That army crossed the Rhine and liberated Europe in 1945; that army amphibiously assaulted countless Japanese-held islands in the Pacific. Had that army with its massive power and efficiency remained under arms as a deterrent to communist aggression, there might not have been a Korean War, a Cuban crisis, or a Vietnam. The United States might have realized a *Pax Americana*, a tranquil period akin to the *Pax Romana*, "Roman peace," the longest duration of peace and prosperity in world history.[34]

---

33. Brinton, Christopher, and Wolff, eds., *A History of Civilization*, 1:105.

34. Recent scholarship has emphasized that the "limitless majesty of the Roman peace" rested on the might of Roman arms and the collaboration of the propertied classes in all parts of the Empire. Naphtali Lewis and Meyer Reinhold, eds., *Roman Civilization, Sourcebook II: The Empire* (New York: Harper & Row, 1966), 80.

How ironic that something so cruel and brutal as warfare should be the means for preserving freedom and peace, but armies both defend and destroy freedom. Violence is justified as the sole deterrent against violent aggression. If the army of a free nation deters or prevails over an aggressor, freedom is perpetuated and peace reigns.

Military Failure Manifests National Degeneracy

Failure on the battlefield often reflects a general lack of respect for authority and lack of spiritual and establishment incentives among the leaders and people of a nation. Zedekiah and the populace of Judah illustrate this point (2 Chron. 36:11–21; Jer. 34:8–11). Zedekiah had no regard for the spiritual authority of the prophet Jeremiah and disobeyed God's command to "bring its [the nation] neck under the yoke of" (Jer. 27:11), the suzerain, Nebuchadnezzar. The people of Judah had turned away from the Lord, especially in their violation of Deuteronomy 15:12 (cf., Jer. 34:12–16). When the nation denied and flaunted the Word and warnings of God as proclaimed by Jeremiah, the justice of the Lord severely punished Judah for their rampant rebellion against the king of Babylon (Jer. 5:15–17, 21–22; cf., Ps. 119:75; Prov. 3:12; Heb. 12:6). Rebellion against Nebuchadnezzar was rebellion against God (Jer. 27:9–10; 28:16; 38:2–3). The Jewish defeat of 587–586 B.C. can be directly attributed to the defiance of the king and his subjects and their spiritual and moral decline. Rejection of authority and spiritual decay are primary ingredients for military defeat on the battlefield and destruction of personal freedom and national independence.

Only God's grace can deliver a nation in the eleventh hour. Such a deliverance demands the spiritual solution: a resurgence of Bible doctrine resident and functioning in the souls of believers to counteract degeneracy. This does not mean that believers should lay down their arms and look piously heavenward in pseudospiritual entreaty. Christians in a client nation operating on doctrine will never disregard the importance of the military in preserving freedom. They will heed the biblical exhortations that a nation must maintain a strong defense force. Thank God for mature believers and dedicated professional soldiers who persevere in their convictions despite personal pressure, political animosity, and antimilitary sentiment.

Universal Military Training

Success on the battlefield so crucial for national survival requires military training (Num. 31:3–5). Therefore, a maximum number of men in each generation must be comprehensively instructed—instilled with individual and group discipline, team coordination, technical skills, tactical and strategical proficiency. Such intensive training is necessary to develop every soldier's ability to act under the stress of combat. Accomplishing this task demands a faculty of professional officers skilled in the art of war.

> "Or what king, when he sets out to meet another king in battle, will not first sit down and take counsel [with his military staff] whether he is strong [well trained] enough with ten thousand *men* to encounter the one coming against him with twenty thousand?" (Luke 14:31)

Initially, the Jewish client nation subscribed to the concept of universal military training (Num. 1:3 ff.).

> Only in order that the generations of the sons of Israel might be taught war, those who had not experienced it formerly. (Judg. 3:2)

This verse directs that the nation "be taught" how to fight. Wars cannot be won with untrained soldiers. The obligation of a nation dedicated to preserving its sovereignty is to instruct every generation of young men for war. With the passing years, however, Israel lapsed into spiritual decay, idolatry, and moral relativism (Judg. 2:11–23; cf., 17:6), ignoring the army until it virtually ceased to exist and suffering the consequences of military defeat.

A nucleus of professional soldiers, expert in their specialized field, must be perpetuated to school new recruits. Who should serve? The Scripture delineates certain qualifications. War is for adults. In Numbers 1:2–3 and 26:4 God instructed Moses to draft all suitable males twenty years and over for the Israelite army. This establishes the biblical standard for draftees. Several exceptions were noted.

> "When a man takes a new wife, he shall not go out with the army, nor be charged with any duty; he shall be free at home one year and shall give happiness [שָׂמַח, *samach*] to his wife whom he has taken." (Deut. 24:5)

A newly married man should not go to war for the most obvious reason: He cannot concentrate on making war. At this point in life his responsibility is exclusively to "give happiness to his wife." Therefore, "he shall be free [to remain] at home one year." The verb "give happiness," the piel imperative of *samach*, means "to cause his wife to be happy"—to lavish her with undivided attention, engage her in conversation, and make love to her for a year. This initial year of respite and intense concentration on mutual fulfillment christens and bonds the relationship for wonderful years ahead.

> "The officers also shall speak to the people, saying, 'Who is the man that has built a new house and has not dedicated it? [He has a new wife and a new house.] Let him depart and return to his house, lest he die in the battle and another man dedicate it.'" (Deut. 20:5)

A man consumed with love is not focused on military matters. His mental attitude is not conducive to either moral or battle courage. Quite naturally, his beloved bride and his new house captivate his attention. Preoccupied and self-absorbed he would not be an effective part of a combat team. He could easily become a casualty or cause others to become casualties.

> "And who is the man that has planted a vineyard [started a new business] and has not begun to use its fruit? [He has not secured the first year's profits.] Let him depart and return to his house, lest he die in the battle and another man begin to use its fruit." (Deut. 20:6)

A new business also distracts a man from military service. While concentrating on his personal responsibilities, he could not function efficiently as a member of a combat team.

> "And who is the man that is engaged to a woman and has not married her? Let him depart and return to his house, lest he die in the battle and another man marry her." (Deut. 20:7)

A man on the brink of matrimony is, likewise, preoccupied, unable to concentrate in a combat situation. He should be released from military duty as undependable and unstable for the pressure of combat.

"Then the officers shall speak further to the people, and
they shall say, 'Who is the man that is afraid and fainthearted [a coward]? Let him depart and return to his
house, so that he might not make his brothers' hearts melt
like his heart.'" (Deut. 20:8)

The Mosaic Law directed that officers in command of the army determine whether a man was qualified to be a soldier after he had completed basic training. Cowards in the ranks were discharged. In a combat
situation cowardice in a few men can infect an entire unit with unrea-
soning fear. "Fainthearted" recruits had to be discharged to maintain the
morale, effectiveness, and safety of those troops going into battle.

How blessed [אַשְׁרֵי, *'ashere*] are the people who know
the joyful sound [of the trumpet—answering the call
of military training]!
O LORD, they walk [march and advance] in the light [Word of
God] of Thy countenance. (Ps. 89:15)

Great blessing characterizes the nation that continues to respond to
the call of the military bugle. The plural of the Hebrew noun אֶשֶׁר
(*'esher*), "blessed," has a twofold connotation. First, universal military
training raises the quality of young men in any generation. Soldiers
learn self-discipline, team discipline, respect for authority, polish and
poise so necessary in life. Whether the training is used in combat or
not, the discipline, authority orientation, and motivation learned from
military instruction are invaluable for any personal endeavor and for
the stability of the nation in war and peace. Second, when the quality
of the men improve, women and children are blessed by association.
Eligible men must be trained continually and molded into a well-moti-
vated, well-disciplined fighting force ready for war.

DISCIPLINE AND TRAINING ARE OBLIGATORY
FOR EFFECTIVE MILITARY OPERATIONS

The discipline of military training is the dividing line between victory and defeat—the iron in the blood of the soldier that sustains him
through every adverse circumstance of warfare. Discipline and training keep fatigued and hungry troops on their feet and fighting. Discipline and training make bold strategy and timely tactics feasible. A
military machine runs on the fuel of discipline and the mechanics of
training.

The history of warfare does not give the nod to the heaviest battalions but to the best-disciplined and trained battalions. Relying on iron discipline Epaminondas with his few Thebans successfully attacked the mighty Spartan phalanxes on the field of Leuctra (371 B.C.). The steadfast regimen of the Roman legions under the able leadership of Julius Caesar conquered Gaul (58–50 B.C.). A handful of well-schooled Swedes under Gustavus Adolphus vanquished Germany in the Thirty Years War (1618–1648). The disciplined drill of the army of Frederick the Great brought Prussia to the forefront of eighteenth century Europe. The disciplined and unbroken British squares at Waterloo shattered Napoleon's Imperial Army (1815). Without discipline and training no military force can hope for success on the field of battle.

If the manpower of a nation is degenerate and corrupt, crippled by antiauthority attitudes, military training is ineffective. When a nation becomes decadent, it no longer has the means or will to defend itself. The law of volitional responsibility and divine discipline prescribe military defeat,[35] the harbinger of the "fifth cycle of discipline" to a client nation—death, slavery, and dispersion. Not only were the Jews defeated but the Assyrians, Chaldeans, Persians, and Romans were ultimately conquered as their military prowess eroded.

The Jews of the Exodus illustrate the importance of military training. Few men in Israel had military experience during the generations of Egyptian bondage. Moses, Caleb, and Joshua were notable exceptions. When the migrating nation faced combat for the first time (Ex. 17:8–13), Moses ordered Joshua to "choose men for us, and go out, fight against Amalek" (v. 9b). Moses' directive implies that Joshua had formed a cadre to train the Israelites for war during their desert sojourn. Now, Joshua as the commanding general must select those men best prepared to fight. With spiritual encouragement from Moses and training instilled by Joshua the valiant Israelite troops achieved victory over the Amalekites at Rephidim. Schooling in tactics and weaponry was instrumental in preserving the independence of the fledgling nation.

---

35. Under the law of volitional responsibility God mandates that every person be accountable for his decisions and actions (Hosea 8:7a; Gal. 6:7–8a). Likewise, a national entity must take responsibility for the collective decisions and actions of its people. God uses the law of volitional responsibility and divine discipline as wake-up calls to salvation for unbelievers and a painful reminder to believers of His priorities and the importance of spiritual recovery from carnality. See Thieme, *Rebound Revisited* (1995), 16–19.

Leadership and Personal Integrity Are Essential

During training soldiers come to respect unit leaders and adopt their beliefs about how to fight. They also embrace their leader's professional values of loyalty, responsibility, and selfless service. These shared beliefs and values become norms and standards that influence discipline, cohesiveness, and the will to fight.[36]

Military history clearly shows that troops should be trained in tactics and the use of weapons and indoctrinated with essential character traits vital to performance as a soldier: courage, competence, candor, and commitment. These qualities that leadership inculcates by instruction and by example will vastly increase the chances of a unit's effectiveness in crisis situations.

Throughout the course of world history certain nations cultivate excellent military leadership; other nations compile a record of poor military leadership but exhibit a citizenry with exceptional discipline and character. From the time of Frederick William of Prussia, the Great Elector, through World War I (1620–1918) the German army generally exhibited excellent leadership. The officer corps demonstrated phenomenal discipline and intellectual acumen. In the British army junior officers and enlisted men who displayed character, discipline, and fortitude often managed to 'muddle through' the mistakes of their senior commanders. But the principle for military success remains the same. The preservation of freedom depends on the caliber of leadership as well as the discipline displayed by the civilian population, especially those who become soldiers.

> Prepare [military] plans by consultation,
> And make war by wise guidance [of leadership].
> (Prov. 20:18)

Warfare is planned and executed through professional expertise and the astute decisions of leadership. Therefore, the United States must continue to develop military leaders; to cultivate men who can formulate strategic and tactical plans, who can give wise counsel to civilian leaders, who can make war effectively.

---

36. *Field Manual (FM) 22–100, Military Leadership*, (Washington, D. C.: Government Printing Office, October 1983), 82.

Regardless of technical advances, the human element still predominates over the tide of battle. The decisions and actions of individuals remain the fundamental instrument of war. The most indispensable ingredient in preparing and maintaining this human element is leadership, whose requisite integrity results from building certain fundamentals of character.

1. Maturity—the ability to make wise decisions based on reason and moral principle;
2. Will—the perseverance to accomplish a goal, regardless of seemingly insurmountable obstacles;
3. Self-discipline—doing your duty regardless of fatigue or other factors;
4. Flexibility—making timely and appropriate changes in thinking, plans, or methods when you see a better way;
5. Confidence—the assurance to be successful in all endeavors;
6. Endurance—mental, spiritual, and physical stamina;
7. Decisiveness—sound judgment in making good decisions at the proper time;
8. Poise under stress—confident control of emotions under adverse conditions;
9. Initiative—the ability to take action without waiting for orders or supervision;
10. Justice—the fair treatment of all people regardless of race, religion, color, gender, age, or national origin;
11. Self-improvement—the readiness to read, study, seek challenges, and work to strengthen beliefs, values, ethics, knowledge, and skills;
12. Assertiveness—taking charge when necessary;
13. Compassion—sensitivity to the feelings, values, interests, and well-being of others;
14. Sense of humor—not taking yourself too seriously;
15. Creativity—thinking of innovative and better ideas, programs, and solutions to problems;
16. Bearing—posture, overall appearance, and manner of physical movement;
17. Humility—teachability; correcting weaknesses or imperfections in your character, knowledge, and skills.[37]

---

37. These definitions are adapted from *FM 22–100, Military Leadership,* 120–25.

A well-schooled army develops proficient commanders from top to bottom. Competent leadership can attain victory; inept leadership can spell defeat. Bible doctrine in the soul develops and perpetuates the traits of superb leadership.

Spiritual Decline Foreshadows Military Disaster

A progressively feeble military and the subsequent threat to freedom begin with apostasy in the souls of believers. Abandonment of God's truth eroded the spiritual life of the Israelites in the days of the Judges. With spiritual apostasy came a failure to learn the art of war. As a result, the Jews repeatedly became enslaved to other nations.

> "New [false] gods [apostasy] were chosen [by their own
>   volition];
> Then war *was* in the gates.
> Not a shield or a spear was seen
> Among forty thousand in Israel." (Judg. 5:8)

Confronted with conflict, why was Israel not armed for war? Because the military had deteriorated as a result of spiritual desertion. Apostasy always decimates divine viewpoint and the divine establishment attitude of believers.

> Your men will fall by the sword [death in combat],
> And your mighty ones in battle.
> And her gates will lament and mourn;
> And deserted she will sit on the ground. (Isa. 3:25–26)

The result of apostasy is divine discipline in the form of military disaster. Women grieve because husbands, brothers, and sons perish in battle. Cities lie destitute. The civilian populace suffers intensely— women especially are in agony, at the mercy of a rapacious conquering army (Isa. 3:17–24).

> "For the eyes of the LORD move to and fro throughout the
> earth that He may strongly support those whose heart
> [right lobe of the mature believer] is completely His. You
> have acted foolishly in this [apostasy]. Indeed, from now
> on you will surely have wars [divine discipline]."
> (2 Chron. 16:9)

God is on constant reconnaissance to protect and preserve believers operating on divine viewpoint. When enough mature believers exist in a national entity, God also protects and preserves the nation. Believers of a client nation who reject doctrine "will surely have wars" and be defeated.

How does a believer acquire God's viewpoint? Every believer possesses the spiritual apparatus I call "Operation Z" for learning, understanding, and applying Bible doctrine. Operation Z is empowered by means of the filling of the Holy Spirit, acquired at salvation and maintained through the rebound technique (1 John 1:9),[38] in conjunction with the human spirit

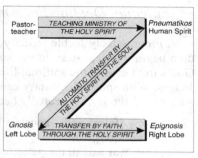

(1 Cor. 2:11–12; cf., Heb. 4:12), also acquired at regeneration. Initially, Bible doctrine is communicated by a pastor-teacher to the human spirit through the teaching ministry of the Holy Spirit (John 16:13). This spiritual phenomena, πνευματικός (*pneumatikos* in the Greek of 1 Cor. 2:13), transfers from the human spirit to the left lobe νοῦς (*nous*) or staging area of the soul as academic knowledge, γνῶσις (*gnosis*).

At this point, volition must be exercised. If the doctrine in the left lobe is believed, then the Holy Spirit transfers that doctrine into the right lobe of the soul. As a result of this spiritual metabolism,[39] doctrine resides in the right lobe and becomes ἐπίγνωσις (*epignosis*) or "full knowledge" (Eph. 3:19). Only *epignosis* doctrine has spiritual value and can be applied to the circumstances of life. New norms and standards form as a result of this divine viewpoint.

The right lobe is the key to divine viewpoint, discernment, application of doctrine to experience, and divine wisdom that preserve a nation (Isa. 33:6). No believer can glorify God or be the salt that preserves a

---

38. See section on Rebound, 69. See also Thieme, *Rebound & Keep Moving!* (1993).

39. Metabolism is derived from the classical Greek noun μεταβολή (*metabole*), meaning "metamorphosis" or "transformation." When food is consumed, the human body converts it into nourishment for physical growth and eliminates harmful waste material. By analogy, when Bible doctrine, spiritual food, is 'eaten' under the filling of the Holy Spirit, it is converted to nourishment for spiritual growth and eliminates human viewpoint in the Christian life (Jer. 15:16a).

nation (Matt. 5:13) apart from Bible doctrine metabolized and resident in the right lobe of the soul.

> For this reason also, since the day we heard *of it*, we have not ceased to pray for you and to ask that you may be filled with the [*epignosis*] knowledge of His will in all spiritual wisdom and understanding, so that you may walk in a manner worthy of the Lord, to please *Him* in all respects, bearing fruit in every [divine] good work and increasing in the [*epignosis*] knowledge of God. (Col. 1:9–10)

The will of God is contained in Bible doctrine, but the full knowledge of His will can only be realized through the daily function of Operation Z.

Mature believers who possess divine viewpoint from metabolized doctrine can reverse the decline of a client nation. Such believers held back the destruction of Judah during the Sennacherib invasion (701 B.C.). Isaiah had been teaching Bible classes for a year before the Assyrians attacked Judah. Those who matured under Isaiah's ministry manned the ramparts, unafraid of Assyrian threats (Isa. 36:20–21). God honored their faith and confounded the most powerful empire of the day (Isa. 37:36–37).

The same is true for believers in any era of history. A few believers with doctrine in the early Church turned the world upside down (Acts 17:6). Likewise, believers who consistently utilize Operation Z remain the only hope to counter the continuing decline of the United States of America. Christians carry in their soul a bastion against every threat to a client nation.

THE DIVINE SOLUTIONS

The faithfulness of a nation to the laws of divine establishment and the dedication of believers to Bible doctrine are the divine solutions that guarantee freedom in an ominous and belligerent world. Throughout history nations sign and ratify treaties to maintain peace and freedom, but alliances never guarantee an end to hostility. Treaties are only as good as the integrity of the nations that sign the pact. Neither can any international organization underwrite freedom nor peace anywhere in the world. Why? The fundamental depravity of the human race since the fall of Adam prevents the abolition of war.

> What is the source of quarrels and conflicts [wars] among
> you? Is not the source your pleasures [the activity of the
> sin nature] that wage war in your members? You lust and
> do not have; *so* you commit murder. And you are envious
> and cannot obtain; *so* you fight and quarrel. (James 4:1–2*a*)

The antagonist is the sin nature; the culprit is man's volition. Since man
never loses the sin nature during his lifetime and continues to make un-
wise or wicked decisions (1 John 1:8, 10), conflict will continue until
the Lord returns. The solution begins with the spiritual life of the believer and adherence to establishment principles by the unbeliever.

Spiritual Life and Establishment Laws

God in His grace has appointed two restraints for the sin nature in
order to guarantee the survival of the human race, promote the progress
of history, and secure God's final victory in the angelic conflict at the
second advent of Jesus Christ. The first restraint is spiritual—
regeneration and the spiritual life.

> "Unless one is born again [regenerated], he cannot see the
> kingdom of God." (John 3:3*b*)

Neither rationalism, empiricism, the intellectual prowess of mankind,
nor good works can bring humanity into the presence of the living God.
Mankind cannot solve the problem of sin or earn eternal life. There is no
human solution, only the divine solution—faith alone in Jesus Christ
alone. He is God's eternal Son who died as a substitute for our sins and
rose from the dead for our justification (Rom. 4:25; 5:8, 18).

> For no man can lay a foundation other than the one which
> is laid, which is Jesus Christ. (1 Cor. 3:11)

Man's foundation of wealth, intellect, and power is temporary and
insecure; God's foundation, the rock Jesus Christ, is abiding, immov-
able, ageless. The attacks of intellectualism will not crumble this foundation; the acid of ridicule will not dissolve this foundation; God's
judgment against sin and national degeneracy will not fall upon this
foundation.

> "And there is salvation in no one else; for there is no other
> name [Jesus Christ] under heaven that has been given
> among men, by which we must be saved." (Acts 4:12)

"Believe in the Lord Jesus, and you shall be saved." (Acts 16:31*b*)

After regeneration, the believer must allow the Holy Spirit to control his life (Gal. 5:16). Only in the power of the Spirit can the believer grow (2 Pet. 3:18), serve, and glorify God. The Holy Spirit fills the believer (Eph. 5:18) to provide the dynamics for living the spiritual life and to nullify the control of the sin nature.[40]

The second restraint of the sin nature is the laws of divine establishment including government that supports:

1. A strong and resolute military with a grand strategy to protect freedom from enemies outside the nation;
2. Vigorous law enforcement and objective jurisprudence to protect freedom from enemies inside the nation.

The sin nature is not only the source of war, but also the source of crime. Both war and crime have been scourges to mankind through the ages. God ordained the military for protection from external aggression and law for protection from internal aggression. The stability of a nation depends on a powerful and proficient military organization, a fair and objective body of laws, and impartial, uncompromising enforcement of those laws.

Both the military and law enforcement share one common goal: defeat the enemy, both foreign and domestic. The military must deter or crush the foreign enemy while the judicial system must deter, incarcerate or execute the criminal (Ex. 21:23; cf., Rom. 13:4). Only then can the specter of tyranny and anarchy be dissipated and peace and freedom be assured.

When flawed leadership and subjective interpretation of law neutralize the effectiveness of the military and law enforcement, the probability of war intensifies and the crime rate soars. The nation is victimized when the military is neglected, despised, ineffective; honest citizens are victimized by criminals. The duty of divinely ordained government is to secure freedom by promoting a strong defense against all enemies.

The laws of divine establishment are designed to protect citizens, to protect property, and to give equal opportunity for all to pursue a

---

40. Thieme, *Old Sin Nature vs. Holy Spirit* (1988); *Rebound & Keep Moving!*

course in life. Freedom provides the environment to succeed or to fail based on one's own motivation, decisions, and capabilities. Decisions and actions precipitate a diversity of results. No two people succeed to the same degree, and no two equally fail. Hence, the blessings of freedom guarantee inequality among people. Those in governing authority must support equality of opportunity to flourish or falter, but never coerce equality of results.

Equality is unattainable for human beings apart from faith in Jesus Christ. At the moment of salvation all believers share an equal position and destiny in Christ. The Savior also secures equal opportunity by providing equal assets for spiritual advance during the lifetime of the believer and an eternal future in heaven.

God always gives the human race a 'fair shake' in every generation. No one reaches the age of accountability without having the opportunity to be saved.[41] The realization of our insignificance compared to the absolute power and righteousness of the Creator of the universe is the point of God-consciousness. Sooner or later, all normal members of the human race reach this point. At that time, a person will be either positive or negative toward God. Should anyone seek the truth and desire a relationship with God, He has promised to provide the information and opportunity to hear the Gospel (Acts 8:26–34). Anytime an unbeliever desires the truth, that person will be exposed to the Gospel message. Because of the grace of God in providing salvation through Jesus Christ to anyone who seeks the Savior, there are countless people in heaven. Because of the laws of divine establishment, the human race has been perpetuated so that people may exercise freedom to make the decision to believe in Jesus Christ.

Whereas in the past, patriotism, morality, and individual sacrifice characterized the American way of life, today such qualities are exceptions rather than the rule. Multitudes of people refuse to assume the responsibilities of citizenship in a free nation. Influenced by relativism and secularism they have no clearly defined objectives other than instant gratification and self-aggrandizement. Successive generations of Americans are progressively abandoning the principles which established and preserved this nation. In this fertile soil of unrealistic

41. The age of accountability is the point at which a person becomes conscious of God, a recognition of the possibility of the existence of a supreme being, and is able to comprehend the Gospel. See Thieme, *Heathenism*, 18–23; also *Witnessing* (1992), 14.

expectations, spiritual and moral decline, and lack of a personal and national destiny are sown the seeds of disaster and slavery.

> Listen to the word of the LORD, O sons of Israel,
> For the LORD has a case against the inhabitants of the land,
> Because there is no faithfulness [truth] or kindness [loyalty]
> Or knowledge of God in the land.
> *There is* swearing, deception, murder, stealing, and
>   adultery.
> They employ violence [crime], so that bloodshed follows
>   bloodshed.
> Therefore the land mourns,
> And everyone who lives in it languishes. (Hosea 4:1–3*a*)

We have seen that freedom cannot survive spiritual and moral decline that devalue and deteriorate the national defense. When degeneracy and decay weaken the undergirding of virtue and integrity, God is neglected, freedom is taken for granted, and the military is ridiculed and despised.

> God and the soldier we adore
> In time of danger—not before
> The danger past and all things sighted
> God is forgotten and the soldier slighted.[42]

Despite scorn from those who are recipients of freedom courtesy of the military, the profession of arms is honorable before God and all who understand the principles of divine establishment. The soldier may be unappreciated or even detested by those he is called upon to defend, yet his duty to God and country remains. Through the fog of national confusion and decadence there shines in the souls of a dedicated few the lucid light of Bible doctrine and the common sense of divine establishment.

---

42. Unknown soldier in the army of the Duke of Marlborough.

Part Two

TO THE SOLDIER

THE CHRISTIAN SOLDIER

CAN A BELIEVER IN JESUS CHRIST serve his country as a soldier, kill the enemy, and at the same time be a good Christian? Can a believer justify being a conscientious objector? Did God contradict Himself in the commandments, "You shall not murder" (Ex. 20:13) and "You shall defeat them, then you shall utterly destroy them [annihilate every man, woman, and child]" (Deut. 7:2b)?

Before these questions can be resolved, we must first remember that two kingdoms coexist on earth today: the spiritual kingdom of believers in Jesus Christ, the Church, and the earthly kingdom of believers and unbelievers, citizens of a national entity, the state. The Scripture categorizes spiritual principles for Christ's kingdom and divine establishment principles for the earthly kingdom. The Lord Himself confirmed the existence of these two realms and the responsibility of the believer to fulfill his duty to both when He said,

> "Render to Caesar [earthly kingdom] the things that are Caesar's; and to God [spiritual kingdom] the things that are God's." (Matt. 22:21b)

The believer's duties to the state are compatible with his duties to God. Both realms are to be coordinated but never combined. The preeminent responsibility of the Christian is to God: study His Word, learn promises, techniques, and doctrines, grow spiritually (2 Pet. 3:18), worship, witness, pray. Only then can the believer render "to God the things that are God's." Yet, the believer also has a responsibility to the state as a citizen—to obey the law, vote, pay taxes, heed the call of jury duty, serve in the government, and as a soldier defend the nation against foreign aggression. This merging of civic and military responsibility is eloquently expressed in "The American's Creed."

> I believe in the United States of America, as a government of the people, by the people, for the people; whose just powers are derived from the consent of the governed; a democracy in a Republic; a sovereign Nation of many sovereign States; a perfect Union, one and inseparable; established upon those principles of freedom, equality, justice and humanity for which American patriots sacrificed their lives and fortunes. I therefore believe it is my duty to my country to love it, to support its Constitution, to obey its laws, to respect its flag, and to defend it against all enemies.[43]

In accepting a commission on 29 May 1940 as a second lieutenant in the United States Army I took an oath—the same one that every officer in the military has taken since the inception of our armed forces.

> I do solemnly swear that I will support and defend the constitution of the United States against all enemies, foreign or domestic, that I will bear true faith and allegiance to the same, that I take this obligation freely without any mental reservation or purpose of evasion: and that I will well and faithfully discharge the duties of the office upon which I am about to enter: so help me God.

This affirmation has in no way conflicted with my obligation to the Lord Jesus Christ. I have, therefore, never deviated from my responsibility. I believe as strongly in the tenets of this oath today as I did in 1940. I do not think any Christian should repudiate the duty of defending his country. A believer's spiritual responsibility to serve the Lord is never an excuse to shirk his civil or military responsibility to serve his nation.

The particulars of soldiering—close order drill, weapons instruction, tactical coordination, leadership training, learning how to fight—are all skills to be mastered. God sanctions military training (Ps. 18:34, 37–40).

---

43. "The American's Creed" by William Tyler Page was adopted by an Act of Congress, 6 April 1918.

But no biblical support or divine approval exists for the conscientious objector. Believers who avoid military service are not only carnal but can bring the wrath of God on the entire nation (Num. 32:6–15).

> "But if you will not do so [not go to war], behold, you
> have sinned against the LORD, and be sure your sin [of
> cowardice] will find you out [personal and national reper-
> cussions]." (Num. 32:23)

Confusion among Christians about fighting for freedom originates from ignorance of divine viewpoint and ignorance of history. The Bible cites numerous instances of national freedom and autonomy gained and maintained by the military victories of Israel verifying that war is morally justifiable. Though immoral acts may be committed by individual soldiers, the underlying principle of national defense is not negated. Killing the enemy in combat is not sinful. "You shall not murder" (לֹא תִרְצָח, *lo tirtzach*) refers *only* to the criminal act of homicide, not taking the life of enemy soldiers in legitimate warfare.

> Then Jesus said to him [Peter], "Put your sword back into
> its place; for all those who take up the sword shall perish
> by the sword." (Matt. 26:52)

This verse is often mistaken as an antiwar declaration. But the context in which Jesus spoke was not at all related to military activities. Taking up the sword refers to the crime of homicide; perishing by the sword refers to capital punishment for that homicide. Consequently, this statement of our Lord does not justify or permit conscientious objection to military service.

> Blessed be the LORD, my rock,
> Who trains my hands for war,
> *And* my fingers for battle. (Ps. 144:1)

David, the magnificent warrior king of Israel, began life as a shepherd, untrained for war. In this serene isolation he grew to spiritual maturity. Then came the opportunity to exhibit his spiritual adulthood as he observed Israel's army cowering in the presence of Goliath, the Philistine giant. With courage forged from absolute confidence in the Lord, David killed the arrogant challenger in single combat. Only later did he learn the art of war from God (2 Sam. 22:35). When war is legitimate, killing is necessary (2 Sam. 22:40–41); when it is not legitimate, then killing becomes homicide.[44] God never teaches or condones murder.

Part of the Christian serviceman's witness is to be the best possible soldier as unto the Lord, including killing the enemy in combat. Many Christians served the Roman Empire in Caesar's legions while also serving as witnesses for Jesus Christ to their fellow soldiers and the nation. A dramatic incident occurred in A.D. 174 when a Roman detachment including the 6th legion, known as the "Thunderbolts," was ambushed by barbarians. The Romans were surrounded, cut off, wounded, and tortured by thirst. The barbarians held off the final assault thinking that the exhausted legion would surrender. Suddenly a thunderstorm burst over the field. Catching the rain in their shields and helmets the Roman legionaries revived themselves and their horses. Revitalized, they routed the enemy.

> It happened that the legion [6th] in question, which came from Cappadocia, was composed of Christians. This is the first mention we have of Christian soldiers being victorious as such. . . . That it was really due to the constancy of the Christians, who, as so often, were ready to face death rather than betray their faith and loyalty be it to Caesar or to Christ, is the underlying truth of the matter. . . . The incident itself made such an impression that it is represented on Marcus' column in Rome.[45]

None could doubt the loyalty and steadfastness of these soldiers serving Christ and Caesar. They made a conspicuous contribution for the cause of their Savior, as well as for the cause of their country. A Christian should also be a patriot!

The Honorable Military

For half a century I have taught the concept of freedom through military victory. Why? To reveal the biblical viewpoint on warfare and to encourage those who serve to appreciate the honorable nature of their calling. Each individual entering the military willingly sacrifices

---

44. Acts of terrorism are not part of legitimate warfare, cannot be justified as an extension of legitimate warfare, and are never sanctioned by God.

45. Stewart Perowne, *Caesars and Saints* (New York: W. W. Norton & Co., 1963), 40.

personal independence and submits to a strict system of discipline while preparing to defend the freedom of his countrymen. This service may culminate in the ultimate sacrifice of his life. The nobility of this dedication conveys the utmost in honor.

Any national crisis that involves American troops serves as a reminder that military service is indispensable, as well as bona fide Christian service. God's plan calls for believers with doctrine in their soul to defend the four divine institutions. Those who wear the uniform of the Army, the Navy, the Marine Corps, the Air Force, or the Coast Guard represent the principle of sustaining freedom through military victory.

PROTECTION FOR THE CHRISTIAN SOLDIER

Since military service is honorable before the Lord, God protects those He honors. Omnipotent God is able to safeguard the believer even in a perilous battlefield environment. The Christian warrior must trust in "the Mighty Fortress," Jesus Christ, and make the Lord of hosts his "stronghold."

> The nations made an uproar [went to war], the kingdoms tottered;
> He [the Lord] raised His voice, the earth melted.
> The LORD of hosts [the armies] is with us;
> The God of Jacob is our stronghold. Selah.
> Come, behold the works of the LORD,
> Who has wrought desolations in the earth. (Ps. 46:6–8)

When the psalmist urges, "Come, behold the works of the Lord," he is instructing believing soldiers of a client nation to watch the Lord's preserving grace sustain them in time of war. Jesus Christ controls every aspect of history including warfare. What a secure bulwark is the Lord of the armies who "is with" believers in action. If He imposes "desolations in the earth," He can quite easily guide the destiny of those in the life and death conditions of combat.

> He makes wars to cease to the end of the earth;
> He breaks the bow and cuts the spear in two;
> He burns the chariots with fire. (Ps. 46:9)

Cast your burden upon the LORD, and He will sustain you;
He will never allow the righteous to be shaken.
But Thou, O God, wilt bring them down to the pit of
    destruction;
Men of bloodshed and deceit will not live out half their
    days.
But I will trust in Thee. (Ps. 55:22–23)

Who [believers] are protected by the power of God
through faith for a salvation ready to be revealed in the
last time. (1 Pet. 1:5)

God promises judgment on any hostile nation that draws a sword
against a client nation and rescue for the nation that observes the laws
of divine establishment and has a pivot of mature believers. Likewise,
God promises to care for the believer through the ordeal of warfare.
The individual believer must trust in the deliverance of the Lord, a
faith that is never misplaced.

One unfailing weapon possessed by the Christian warrior is
prayer—the prayer for protection.

Rescue me, O LORD, from evil men;
Preserve me from violent men,
Who devise evil things in *their* hearts;
They continually stir up wars. (Ps. 140:1–2)

In modern warfare a successful tactical operation is prefaced with a
barrage of artillery. When artillery fire pins down, disorganizes, con-
fuses, or routs the enemy, casualties are minimized and battles are
won. One of the greatest weaknesses of the Church today is the lack of
a prayer barrage—prevailing prayer.[46] Prayer is every believer's means
of direct petition to God the Father for logistical and fire support in
the advance of the Christian life. We are commanded to "pray without
ceasing" (1 Thess. 5:17)—to pray consistently. I stand as a recruiting
officer looking for faithful prayer warriors to enlist in the Lord's Artillery. In the privacy of our royal priesthood pray for those encountering
combat pressure.

---

46. Thieme, *Prayer* (2003), 18–22.

Our gracious Heavenly Father, we pray for our men and women who are on active duty. Many of them are in places of great danger and we recognize the fact that they have a testimony for You and the most wonderful opportunity to apply doctrine and become stalwart Christian warriors. We not only pray for them but also for those many, many more who will be called to the colors. We ask that they might fulfill the very purpose for which they have been graced out all of these years in learning and using Bible doctrine. We pray that we might be faithful on our part in the perception of doctrine so that we can become part of the pivot that will inevitably result in victory for our nation.

We are grateful, Heavenly Father, that we live in a time that there is such a challenge—not just a military challenge but a challenge to face so many different kinds of adversities; a challenge related to the fact that client nation USA is under fire in so many ways. We pray that through all the confusion that is going to exist in the future, through all the adversities that will come our way, that we will glorify Thee so that in Thy perfect will and in Thy perfect plan when each one of us is called home, we might hear that wonderful phrase: "Well done, good and faithful servant; you have been faithful over a few things, I will make you ruler over many things." We ask all this in the name of our Lord and Savior Jesus Christ. Amen.[47]

THE VIRTUE OF THE CHRISTIAN SOLDIER

The soldier who concentrates on his duty under the pressure of combat will manifest the fortitude and resourcefulness necessary to accomplish his mission and survive. The Christian warrior who concentrates on the promises and doctrines of the Word of God gains absolute confidence in God's everlasting care (Matt. 6:25–27; 1 Pet. 5:7), shows his mettle, endures adversity, and secures deliverance. In life and in death the Lord always delivers (Phil. 1:21). Consequently, valor requires concentration on the Lord Jesus Christ as demonstrated in the mandate from the Mosaic Law to never fear a numerically superior enemy.

---

47. A prayer offered in Berachah Church, 24 August 1990.

"When you go out to battle against your enemies and see
horses and chariots *and* people more numerous than you,
do not be afraid of them; for the LORD your God [Jesus
Christ], who brought you up from the land of Egypt, is
with you." (Deut. 20:1)

Deuteronomy 20:1 was addressed to the client nation Israel. The
Jewish infantry was the finest in the world but Israel did not possess
cavalry or a chariot corps. What was the mandate from God to the out-
manned, underequipped Jews? "Do not be afraid of them." The Lord
exhorted these Jews to concentrate on Him, not on the enemy; to keep
their eyes on the solution, not on the problem. Remembering His faithfulness in a past crisis inspires courage and assures deliverance in the
present crisis. God had brought them "up from the land of Egypt" and
delivered them at the Red Sea and He would deliver them now. In
eternity past He made provision for all their needs and problems. They
must trust and concentrate on His resources.

Likewise, God makes the same provision for every believer in client nation USA. As a soldier fighting for your country, remember that
this mandate and promise to Israel is a mandate and promise for you.
God is gracious and steadfast in delivering His people—whether in a
nation of confused, complaining, carnal believers like ancient Israel or
like the United States today. When a few magnificent Christian warriors hold the line for Bible doctrine and divine establishment, God will
honor those men and bless the nation with victory.

"Now it shall come about that when you are approaching
the battle, the priest shall come near and speak to the people." (Deut. 20:2)

At the time this verse was written the armies of Israel were encouraged first by their national leader, Moses, father of the first Jewish client
nation, then by their spiritual leaders, members of the Levitical priesthood. These priests delivered a message of confidence and courage.
Communicators of God's Word have a spiritual responsibility to instill
moral and battle courage.

In the Church Age believers live in the dispensation of a universal
"royal priesthood" (1 Pet. 2:9). You are your own priest. Your confidence and courage must originate from the metabolized doctrine resident in your soul. The key to successful military action is spiritual
strength. I would expect believer-priests with doctrine in their soul to

approach a campaign with the same bravery summoned by the Levitical priests.

> "Hear, O Israel, you are approaching the battle against your enemies today. Do not be fainthearted. Do not be afraid, or panic, or tremble before them, for the LORD your God is the one who goes with you, to fight for you against your enemies, to save [deliver] you." (Deut. 20:3b–4)

Today, instead of "Hear, O Israel," we would challenge our soldiers: "Hear, O Christian warrior, you will soon meet the enemy in battle. Do not be afraid; do not panic; do not tremble before them, for Jesus Christ is the one who accompanies you against the enemy, to deliver you." Obeying these three vital mandates instills courage in the believer facing battle.

1. *Do not be fainthearted; do not be afraid.* Dread affects your will and effectiveness to fight. During the War Between the States, the Union General George McClellan allowed fear to cloud his mind in the heat of battle.

> He would believe incorrectly that he was vastly outnumbered, and he would withdraw. At these crucial moments in history, his character failed to control his fears and keep his mind clear to see and deal with reality.[48]

When you faithfully metabolize and apply the Word of God, you suppress anxiety. By controlling this heart-pounding reaction you keep your thoughts and energy focused on doing your duty. Your spiritual concentration rouses strength of character. You are able to stabilize under pressure. Promises and doctrines from God's Word replace fear and stress with calm and poise (2 Tim. 1:7).

> "Be strong and courageous, do not be afraid or tremble at them, for the LORD your God is the one who goes with you. He will not fail you or forsake you." (Deut. 31:6)

---

48. *FM 22–100, Military Leadership,* 173.

This commission from God is directed to you as a soldier. "Strong" refers to the power of the spiritual life derived from metabolized doctrine; "courageous" refers to the expression of this spiritual strength. "Be strong and courageous" is a mandate to possess and display moral courage that originates from spiritual strength. Moral courage overcomes any apprehensions you may have while doing what ought to be done.[49] Moral courage demands standing firm on convictions drawn from virtue and values from metabolized doctrine resident in your soul.

"Do not be afraid" is a divine mandate for battle courage—overcoming fears of bodily harm while doing your duty.[50] How? Spiritual strength generates not only moral courage but also battle courage. This dual courage allows you to remember your training and operate your weapon expertly during the adversity of combat. You do not morbidly dwell on the possibility of personal injury or death.

2. *Do not panic.* The sudden emergence of irrational, emotional terror paralyzes thought and action. Encouragement from doctrine quells this panic and elicits battle courage. Tranquillity under pressure is the overt expression of a courageous soul.

"The Lord your God is the one who goes with you. He will not fail you or forsake you" (Deut. 31:6b), is assurance that the Lord Jesus Christ Himself will never desert you in battle or anywhere else. Panic vanishes in the confidence of His ever-present protection—He is your 'point man.' This foremost position is the most dangerous when advancing toward the enemy. The individual, the squad, the platoon, or the company in the vanguard are first to meet the enemy and receive fire. In so doing they offer early warning and protection for the main body of troops. Deuteronomy 31:8 clearly identifies the Lord as our point.

> "And the LORD is the one who goes ahead of you
> [as the point]; He will be with you. He will not fail
> you or forsake you. Do not fear, or be dismayed."
> (Deut. 31:8)

---

49. Ibid., 90.
50. Ibid.

3. *Do not tremble.* Fear causes debilitating physical reactions. Rising tension shakes a soldier like the passage of a powerful electric current. But by fixing your thinking on divine viewpoint, you alleviate the instinctual reactions of anxiety and fear and ensure the physical control of your body. The resulting battle courage may not eliminate fear but allows you to put your training in action in spite of it.[51] With focus and fortitude from Bible doctrine you will recall your training and execute your mission under adverse conditions.

Professionalism

Killing the enemy in battle is neither immoral nor sinful (Deut. 20:13). The believer, filled with the Holy Spirit, motivated by metabolized doctrine in his soul, and obedient to the orders of his superiors should calmly and efficiently plan and execute the destruction of the enemy. When a soldier on the battlefield follows the principles set down by Deuteronomy 20:3 and Psalm 144:1 and gains control of his mind and body, he demonstrates personal responsibility and nobility of character, symbolizes selfless service, and competently executes his duties; in a word, he exhibits professionalism.

Professionalism demands recall and application of the training that prepared your mind and body to function normally in the abnormal circumstances of war. If you convert the outside pressure of adversity into the inner pressure of stress in the soul, the mental application of your training becomes impossible. Your power of execution comes from spiritual strength. With doctrine circulating in your soul you have the grit to concentrate under combat pressure.

Deuteronomy 20:3–4; 31:6, 8 should be metabolized by every Christian warrior. If I were a chaplain, I would address similar words to troops before they enter combat. Since I cannot be with you to prompt concentration and courage, to comfort and encourage, I urge you to saturate your soul with divine viewpoint from the unfailing, infallible Word of God before you face the crisis. The Lord is your comfort and ever-present help in time of trouble (Ps. 46:1). Bible doctrine steadies you under pressure situations and instills motivation for a professional attitude of confidence and calm resolution.

---

51. Ibid., 138.

Though a host [an army] encamp against me,
My heart will not fear;
Though war arise against me,
In *spite of* this I shall be confident. (Ps. 27:3)

Victory over Fear—The Ten Problem-Solving Devices

The United States Army employs the acronym FLOT, Forward Line of Troops, to designate front line units in the defense that will encounter and do battle with the enemy. They deny the adversary access to specific terrain for a specified time and slow, canalize, and defeat the enemy's major units.[52] God has provided for you a spiritual FLOT, a defense line in your soul to meet and defeat the enemies of the spiritual life. The line consists of ten combat units, problem-solving devices that reinforce and strengthen as you grow to spiritual maturity. This battle line delivers victory in four intense conflicts: the temptations of the sin nature, the pressure of stress in the soul, the allure of false doctrine, and the tendency to trust in human solutions. By deploying God's defense system you guarantee ultimate triumph against encroachment to your spiritual life.

The problem-solving devices are the God-given means of accurate and correct application of doctrine to experience. They prevent the inevitable outside pressures of adversity from overwhelming your soul. Operation of these devices begins with your recovery from carnality. Restored to fellowship with God your spiritual life is empowered for advance. As you acquire *epignosis* knowledge, you incorporate the problem-solving mechanics for leading a life of meaning, purpose, definition, and fulfillment of God's plan. Whether surrounded by adversity or prosperity, you can solve every human problem by deploying the appropriate combination of these ten devices.

#1: REBOUND

When your soul is controlled by the sin nature, you are carnal and powerless to live the spiritual life (Rom. 7:15–21). Rebound is the *only* solution to carnality and the *only* problem-solving device that

---

52. *FM 100–5, Operations* (5 May 1986), 137.

functions in a state of sin. How do you recover from carnality? Simply name your personal sins privately to God the Father.

> If we confess [name] our [known] sins, He is faithful and righteous to forgive us our [known] sins and to cleanse [purify] us from all [unknown or forgotten sins] unrighteousness. (1 John 1:9)

The mechanics of recovery from sin are fourfold: (1) Name the sin to immediately receive complete divine forgiveness and to reestablish the absolute status of spirituality, the control of your soul by the Holy Spirit; (2) isolate the sin to stop any bitterness (Heb. 12:15); (3) forget the sin so as not to reclaim guilt (Phil. 3:13); (4) keep moving in the spiritual life (Phil. 3:14).

Remorse is not a prerequisite for this recovery technique. Rebound purifies you from all unrighteousness, restoring fellowship with God the Father so that you can resume living the spiritual life. The only way you can employ the nine remaining problem-solving devices or fulfill God's plan for your life is through the ministry of the Holy Spirit regained from rebound.

#2: THE FILLING OF THE HOLY SPIRIT

The Holy Spirit empowers you to apply Bible doctrine, execute God's plan, become an invisible hero, and glorify God by utilizing all the assets He has provided. Accordingly, you are mandated to "be filled with the Spirit" (Eph. 5:18b). This filling that controls your soul after rebound energizes the problem-solving devices and supports your resistance to the temptations of the sin nature.

> But I say, walk by [means of] the Spirit, and you will not carry out the desire of the flesh [sin nature]. (Gal. 5:16)

In carnality, grieving and quenching the Holy Spirit, your advance halts—you cannot grow spiritually, resist the temptations from the lust patterns and trends of the sin nature, or use the divine problem-solving devices. But from the filling of the Holy Spirit comes the source of the spiritual life. Under His mentorship you can "walk by the Spirit"—learn the Word of God (John 16:13) and apply Bible doctrine to circumstances.

The filling of the Holy Spirit converts the lowest human IQ into spiritual IQ. Every believer now has equal opportunity and equal privilege to perceive and understand Bible doctrine which forms and operates the eight remaining problem-solving devices in the soul.

#3: THE FAITH-REST DRILL

When you are so beset by difficulties that you cannot think clearly, you must apply the most basic form of doctrine, the promises of God. Promises urge you to cultivate a persistent and habitual trust in God, which the Bible calls "persevering" or patience (Rom. 12:12). Patience means you are steadfast in *believing* God's Word. When you are under pressure, adversity, disaster, and have hit a dead end, you must cling to God's promises until they become more real to you than your situation, experience, or emotions. When faith in the promises permeates your soul, you can *rest* in the tranquillity and contentment acquired from divine viewpoint.

A promise is a divine guarantee, a capsule statement of doctrine, a solid rock upon which to anchor your mental attitude. Promises express the essence and policy of God, provide instantaneous perspective, and reduce complicated situations to their utmost simplicity. Numerous promises in the Bible express the perpetual logistical support and care of God and assure us of His unlimited ability to help in time of need.

The steps for using the faith-rest drill are: (1) Claim a promise to stabilize your soul; (2) glean from that promise a relevant doctrine or doctrinal rationale to apply; (3) reach a doctrinal conclusion so that faith is in control of the situation. After employing these three stages you gain immediate divine perspective for the intense pressures of life. Your confidence increases as you use Bible doctrine resident in your soul. Certain of God's steadfastness and secure in His care, you can genuinely rest, relax, and trust in Him for solutions.

> Yet, with respect to the promise of God, he [Abraham] did not waver in unbelief, but grew strong in faith, giving glory to God, and being fully assured that what He had promised, He was able also to perform. (Rom. 4:20–21)

The faith-rest drill stabilizes your mentality, regains your ability to think under pressure, keeps your emotions in perspective, and reinforces your appreciation of the grace of God (Heb. 4:1–3a; 2 Pet. 1:3–4).

The mixing of faith with promises changes your outlook from one of self-centered arrogance to authority orientation, dignity and poise, teachability, objectivity, and professionalism. Claiming promises becomes an instant reaction force to hold the FLOT line for a time. This faith is the foundation of humility and spiritual strength to execute the plan of God.

#4: GRACE ORIENTATION

Employing the faith-rest drill orients the believer to the grace of God—the firm assurance that you will receive the consideration, equity, and care of the Supreme Court of Heaven. Understanding His grace policy and how little you deserve the incredible bounty He provides motivates humility. Genuine humility in your soul is a system of thinking and a way of life. As a system of thinking, humility is freedom from arrogance and human viewpoint. As a way of life, humility is orientation to authority and to objective reality. Genuine humility creates capacity for greater grace blessings.

> Clothe yourselves with humility toward one another, for GOD IS OPPOSED TO THE PROUD, BUT GIVES GRACE TO THE HUMBLE. Humble yourselves, therefore, under the mighty hand of God, that He may exalt you at the proper time. (1 Pet. 5:5b–6)

In humility you are teachable, your thinking adapts to His grace procedures, you grow spiritually. You realize that only the ability and power of God can meet your needs and provide answers and solutions to the problems of life. Since you are constantly treated with benevolence by the Lord, you begin to apply God's charitable policy of undeserved favor to yourself and others. You become increasingly sensitive to and tolerant of the weaknesses of your fellow man (Eph. 4:31–32). This attitude of grace orientation when linked with metabolizing Bible doctrine produces Christian virtue.

#5: DOCTRINAL ORIENTATION

"For as he thinks within himself, so he is" (Prov. 23:7a). The spiritual life is thinking divine viewpoint and then applying that thinking to your circumstances. When you think with metabolized doctrine, you operate with "the mind of Christ," the only source of absolute wisdom

(1 Cor. 2:16). This orientation permits you to advance from applying the basic promises of spiritual childhood to the complex doctrinal rationales in spiritual adulthood. Doctrine is the glue that holds together all the problem-solving devices on the FLOT line of the soul.

> And do not be conformed to this world, but be transformed by the renewing of your mind [doctrinal orientation], that you may prove what the will of God is, that which is good and acceptable and perfect. For through the grace [orientation] given to me I say to every man among you not to think more highly of himself [humility] than he ought to think; but to think so as to have sound judgment [divine viewpoint], as God has allotted to each a measure of faith [standard of thinking from metabolized doctrine]. (Rom. 12:2–3)

Truth creates a mirror in the soul in which you can accurately and objectively evaluate yourself and your circumstances from divine viewpoint. When you are inculcated with doctrinal norms and standards, you rely on the Lord, make good decisions, and resolve the dilemmas of life God's way.

The objective of the believer's spiritual life is the instilling of truth. But usable *epignosis* doctrine accumulates gradually in increments. Truth builds upon truth. He must persist in learning "line on line, a little here, a little there" (Isa. 28:10). Bit by bit the believer develops a frame of reference for receiving and retaining ever more complex doctrines, thereby unveiling the whole panorama of his magnificent spiritual life. This system explains why the believer must faithfully listen to Bible teaching as a consistent routine and emphasizes the value of repetition by the pastor. Bible doctrine cannot be absorbed and used through sporadic bursts of enthusiasm but through tenacious reception, retention, and recall. The perception and metabolism of Bible doctrine always result in faith, confidence in Christ, and love of God (1 Cor. 13:13) necessary to employ the problem-solving devices of spiritual maturity.

#6: A PERSONAL SENSE OF DESTINY

With confidence from metabolized doctrine in the soul you begin to live in the light of an eternally secure future. Your self-worth becomes inseparably united with Jesus Christ because you eternally share in all that Christ has and is: His righteousness (2 Cor. 5:21), His election (Eph. 1:3–4), His sonship (Gal. 3:26), His priesthood (Heb. 10:10–14), His kingship (2 Tim. 2:11–12), His personal destiny (Rom. 8:30). United with Christ and His destiny you can imitate Him, glorify Him, and you will accompany Him at the Second Advent and rule with Him forever. You have acquired the *sense* of your destiny.

From this realization you attain spiritual self-esteem. With spiritual self-esteem you are able to address and solve problems from the doctrine in your soul, not from the advice of others. You develop the capacity for happiness, for understanding and benefiting from divine blessing, for enduring suffering, for maintaining the momentum of your spiritual life. Never before in history have all these privileges been extended to believers.

> For not one of us lives for himself, and not one dies for himself; for if we live, we live for the Lord, or if we die, we die for the Lord; therefore whether we live or die, we are the Lord's. (Rom. 14:7–8)

Through grace and doctrinal orientation you discern your personal potential in the plan of God. Adversity fades in proximity to the spiritual self-esteem generated from a limitless relationship with the Lord. This authenticated personal destiny weathers all circumstances of adversity or prosperity. When you have a personal recognition of the destiny you share in Christ and the enormity of your spiritual endowment, awe and gratitude toward God animate your attitude.

#7: PERSONAL LOVE FOR GOD THE FATHER

When you discover the perfect essence and integrity of God and the remarkable spiritual assets He has given you, your response of respect, admiration, and reverence fulfills the mandate of Matthew 22:37. Personal love motivates you to conform to the object of your appreciation by following His precedent of virtue and integrity. This motivational virtue based on absolute confidence in the divine ability to care for you supports and sustains momentum for problem-solving and courage in the face of adversity, the same courage expressed in Deuteronomy 31:6, 8.

But how do you love God when the object of your worship and adoration is invisible (1 Pet. 1:8)? You see, know, and love Him only through "truth," Bible doctrine, and "spirit," the filling of the Holy Spirit (John 4:24). When your soul is inculcated with doctrine so that you think His thoughts, share His viewpoint, and appreciate His perfect integrity and matchless grace, you love God. As your capacity to love God increases, you gain confidence that He directs even your problems for your benefit.

> And we know that God causes all things to work together for good to those who *love* God, to those who are called according to *His* purpose. (Rom. 8:28, italics added)

#8: IMPERSONAL LOVE FOR ALL MANKIND

People are among the most severe tests in life. Some of your associations may be thoroughly obnoxious or evil. You want friendship, rapport, or intimacy with only a selected few. Even for these loved ones and close companions a constant personal love is difficult to maintain. There are always times when disappointment, incompatibility, or hostility characterize the most intimate of relationships. How much more impossible it would be to cultivate personal love for the unattractive or unlovable! How, then, can you obey the biblical command to "LOVE YOUR NEIGHBOR AS YOURSELF" (Rom. 13:9b)?

You can only love all people through a mental attitude of impersonal love (Rom. 13:8–10). Impersonal love for the entire human race does not require attraction, friendship, or even acquaintance with the object of love. This unconditional love that flows out of the integrity of the subject rather than the appeal of the object is the same love that God bestows on all unbelievers (John 3:16; Eph. 5:1–2). God planned and executed the salvation of unbelievers based on His perfect integrity. Such love is not sentimental or emotional but virtue-dependent. When you acquire spiritual self-esteem and develop personal love for God (1 John 4:21), you gain the virtue necessary to express impersonal love toward everyone in your periphery.

> Love is patient, love is kind, *and* is not jealous; love does not brag *and* is not arrogant, does not act unbecomingly; it does not seek its own, is not provoked, does not take into account a wrong *suffered*, does not rejoice in unrighteousness, but rejoices with the truth; bears all things, believes all things, hopes all things, endures all things. (1 Cor. 13:4–7)

Impersonal love, derived from divine virtue, takes precedence over the faults and flaws of people. When personal love for God and impersonal love unite to form virtue-love, you will not be encumbered by cruel intolerance, smoldering anger, judging, hatred, or other mental attitude sins, and you will not be distracted by stress, pressure, persecution. You will obey and imitate the Lord by repaying insults and antagonism with compassion, kindness, patience, and humility (Col. 3:12–14; 1 Pet. 3:8–9).

#9: SHARING THE HAPPINESS OF GOD

While suffering the unimaginable agonies of the cross, the humanity of Jesus Christ never lost perfect contentment and joy (Heb. 12:2). His relaxed mental attitude equated adversity with prosperity and living with dying (Phil. 1:21). He never felt threatened or sorry for Himself. His happiness did not change even under difficult circumstances, cruelty, torture, unjust treatment, death. You have access to this same happiness in your life—a beatitude that does not depend upon people, circumstances, or the details of life. When Bible doctrine and virtue-love fill your soul, you will enjoy contentment in the midst of thought, people, system, and disaster testing.

> "These things I [Jesus Christ] have spoken to you [the mandates of Bible doctrine], that My joy [the happiness of God] may be in you, and *that* your joy may be made full [mature and permanent]." (John 15:11)

The happiness of God is enduring and self-sustaining. When your spiritual life takes precedence over circumstances, you carry God's happiness with you as a constant companion. Your divine inner happiness and spiritual maturity conquer any human unhappiness or fearful situations (James 1:2) and generate a tremendous capacity for life. No set of circumstances can defeat you.

#10: OCCUPATION WITH THE PERSON OF JESUS CHRIST

When you intensely love and respect a person, you develop a concentrated ardor for that person. Likewise, when you grow to understand and love the Lord Jesus Christ your attention rivets on Him; He is your role model, the vital pattern for your life. The Lord becomes your closest companion, influencing your every thought and action. You focus moment by moment on Him. Since your spiritual life now depends upon encouragement only from Christ, you cease to depend upon people for love, happiness, help, or support. You have become spiritually self-sustaining. No suffering, disaster, shock, or pressure can intrude on your soul and dim the elucidating presence of the Lord Jesus Christ.

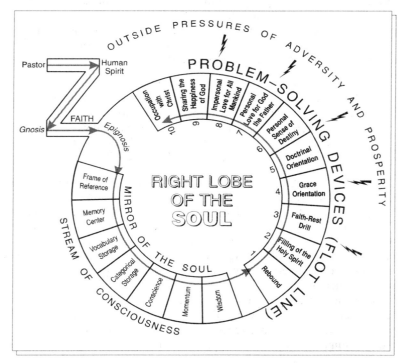

FLOT OF THE SOUL

The key to utilizing this ultimate solution is progressing in spiritual maturity so that the mind of Christ permeates your mind. As you live for Christ, your soul forms the maximum expression of personal love toward God; your priorities conform exclusively to divine viewpoint. Arrogant self-centeredness is replaced by this quintessence of motivation, by an energizing virtue, and by unencumbered enthusiasm and capacity for life. Happiness and contentment characterize your conduct regardless of your circumstances. Problems fade away as the lusts and desires of the sin nature are overruled by your soul's occupation with Christ.

During the Incarnation Jesus Christ displayed impeccable spirituality, faith-rest, grace and doctrinal orientation, fulfillment of His destiny, virtue-love, and the happiness of God. Now, armed with the same power and assets, your mental attitude can reflect His divine problem-solving perspective (2 Cor. 5:14a; 1 Pet. 1:8). The continuous circulation of metabolized Bible doctrine in your soul's stream of consciousness produces a concentration on the Lord that transcends all experiences of living or dying.

> According to my earnest expectation and hope [absolute confidence], that I shall not be put to shame in anything, but *that* with all boldness, Christ shall even now, as always, be exalted in my body, whether by life or by death. For to me, to live is Christ, and to die is gain. (Phil. 1:20–21)

With these problem-solving devices in mind you can focus on resolving the quandary of fear. Courage demands thinking under pressure. The problem-solving devices remove all the cobwebs of fear from your thinking and replace them with a confidence in doctrine which leads to confidence in the Lord. Confident trust in the Lord elicits the highest form of courage—a mental attitude of tranquil composure, thoughtful determination, and stalwart perseverance under every circumstance of life.

You must defeat fear before fear defeats you; only then can you defeat the enemy in battle. When fear strikes, it must not be allowed to ignite a devastating chain reaction of mental attitude sins that incapacitate thinking, decision-making, and actions.

1. The more you surrender to fear, the more you perpetuate fear.
2. The more you perpetuate fear, the greater your capacity for fear.
3. The greater your capacity for fear, the more you increase the power of fear in your life. When you control fear, it has no power in your life.
4. The more you increase the power of fear in your life, the more you live by fear and the greater becomes your failure to learn and utilize Bible doctrine.
5. The more you live by fear the more you are intimidated by life.

6. Fear focuses on the problem, but Bible doctrine focuses on the divine solution. The divine solution is the only solution; human solutions are no solution.
7. Fear is a sin that generates emotionalism, a major distraction to the spiritual life.
8. Fear breeds arrogance, but Bible doctrine nurtures humility and the spiritual life.
9. Fear of death cannot prevent death, but fear can prevent living the spiritual life designed by God for every believer.

Fear epitomizes human viewpoint and obstructs problem solving. Since fear is a component of the emotional complex of sins, it negates thinking, applying doctrine, or any ability to function in a crisis. Unchecked fear neutralizes spiritual FLOT line defenses and destabilizes the mental process. You must recognize the symptoms and effects of fear and vanquish its destructive tendencies. At least five categories of emotional sins stem from the root of fear—worry, hatred, reaction, guilt, self-pity. You must confess, isolate, forget, and move on from these sins to restore battlefield courage and rational thought.[53]

1. Sudden disaster or fear of a future campaign places a soldier under immense pressure and generates *worry, anxiety, panic, loss of control.* Such trepidation squelches the filling of the Holy Spirit and extinguishes the spiritual power supply. As emotions take control of the soul, a soldier becomes a coward. Foreboding replaces objective thinking resulting in an imagination that conjures catastrophic scenarios—a sure formula for retreat and defeat. To recover courage when the stress of fear and worry invades the soul, you must rebound, then use the faith-rest drill. Focus your thinking on a biblical promise and cast your cares upon the Lord (1 Pet. 5:7).

   Be anxious [worry, panic, lose control] for [about] nothing, but in everything by prayer and supplication with thanksgiving let your requests be made known to God. And the peace of God [result of faith-rest drill], which surpasses all comprehension, shall guard your hearts and your minds in Christ Jesus. (Phil. 4:6–7)

---

53. Thieme, *Rebound & Keep Moving!*, 23–24; *Isolation of Sin* (2000), 9–12.

The battle is not yours. The Lord wants you to rely solely on Him. God will faithfully take care of you through all adversity, but the "rest" from faith-rest will not occur until you are filled with the Spirit, claim His promises, and let faith take control of the situation.

When the reality of Bible doctrine confronts the reality of a combat situation, you have a clear choice. If you focus on God's Word, concentration and courage will escort you through the battlefield. If you focus on the problem or the circumstances, worry and anxiety will dog your footsteps. Regardless of the extent of your predicament, faith-rest will work. Bible doctrine in your soul overcomes any difficulty.

For He has delivered me from all trouble;
And my eye has looked *with satisfaction* upon my
    enemies. (Ps. 54:7)

2. A formidable enemy who arouses fear can also inspire intense *hatred*. When a close friend is wounded or killed, the resulting emotional caldron ignites a furious response. Professionalism and objective thinking disappear replaced by loathing and killer lust. These implacable and criminal animosities have no place in a combat situation. Wars are not won by outbursts of emotion, but by composed, measured, deliberate planning and execution.

You must go to war with virtue in your soul: the motivational virtue from personal love for God the Father and the functional virtue of impersonal love for all mankind. The motivational virtue of absolute confidence in God inspires the functional virtue of courage toward man. If you display virtue-love, you cannot simultaneously harbor rage and hatred. You must accomplish your mission dispassionately, remaining within the parameters of the rules of engagement and the conventions of war.

3. Fears that bedevil a soldier facing combat induce *reaction*. This treacherous emotional sin includes bitterness, vindictiveness, implacability. The rampant emotionalism of reaction produces paranoia, increases insecurity, and distorts reality. Reaction promotes self-absorption and self-deception, thereby fragmenting thinking, shattering concentration, and displacing contentment. Prolonged reaction can degenerate to personality dysfunction—neurotic or psychotic behavior. These subjective, introspective,

and irrational responses break down and eliminate virtue and self-discipline so necessary for overcoming the pressure of combat. The believer who refuses to treat a wounded psyche by rebounding and applying the soothing salve of *epignosis* doctrine cannot prevent reaction from escalating to emotional imbalance, mental instability, and egocentricity. What a tragedy to witness this complete divorcement from God's grace.

Humility from grace orientation resists self-centeredness and hypersensitivity and abandons irrationality for sound thinking motivated by doctrinal orientation. You do not succumb to frustration or anger caused by stress, unrealistic expectations, or unjust treatment. Being humble counteracts the false solutions of arrogance, human viewpoint, and the pitfalls of emotionalism (James 4:6). Humility exemplifies the virtue and integrity of the spiritual life.

The Christian soldier also can evade reaction and perpetuate honor and integrity by using impersonal love, the antithesis of bitterness, vindictiveness, implacability. Impersonal love is impervious to hatred, persecution, injustice, or antagonism directed toward you. With impersonal love you no longer lose control of your emotions but impartially and objectively evaluate the conflict swirling around you. Where grace orientation, doctrinal orientation, and impersonal love reside you are unencumbered by sinful reaction.

4. As fear and panic settle in your soul, you may engage in *guilt* to clear your conscience. You immerse yourself in a sea of self-reproach for past failure, for killing the enemy, or the death of a friend. When you are alone with time to think about the destructiveness and desolation of war, you may indulge in morbid recrimination. With unrestrained subjectivity you consider your honorable service shameful and tarnished. Wallowing in guilt, you foster a chain of mental attitude sins that plunge you into reversionism.[54] Each one of these sins is a road to ruin.

Excessive self-reproach prohibits forgetting and isolating sins after rebound and replaces problem-solving devices with defense

---

54. Reversionism is the progressive recession of the believer to the modus operandi of the unbeliever through perpetual carnality and rejection or neglect of Bible doctrine. Reversionism does not imply loss of salvation. See Thieme, *Reversionism* (2000), 13–19.

mechanisms such as repression and denial. Disavowal of painful
or agonizing thoughts, memories, feelings, or impulses only tem-
porarily alleviates guilt and remorse. Such repression collects as
garbage in the subconscious and permits human viewpoint to in-
filtrate and dominate the stream of consciousness. Pangs of inade-
quacy and helplessness intrude on your concentration, evolving
into extreme doubt about the ethics of your endeavor and intense
preoccupation with overtly correct behavior. This tortured state of
mind subverts battle courage. You can no longer have a pro-
ductive spiritual life or be an effective member of a combat team.
   What is God's solution to the sin of guilt?

> Brethren, I do not regard myself as having laid
> hold of *it* yet; but one thing *I do*: forgetting what
> *lies* behind [including guilt] and reaching forward
> to what *lies* ahead. (Phil. 3:13)

Do not dwell obsessively on the past. Never look back—always
look ahead! Killing the enemy in battle is justified and virtuous
before the Lord. Agonizing in quagmires of guilt only bog down
your spiritual advance. Guilt and repression of the past deny the
reality of adversity and quash confidence in divine solutions,
but grace orientation and a personal sense of destiny adjust your
thinking to the reality of divine guardianship. Even in the sur-
realistic circumstance of combat you will embrace the plan of
God rather than seek escape. If you are still alive, God has a
purpose for your life. Leave self-recrimination behind and continue to fulfill your personal spiritual destiny!

5. *Self-pity* frequently occurs in the severe adversity of a combat
   zone. Faced with appalling conditions, a hostile enemy, and an
   uncertain future, morale sinks and you may begin to feel sorry
   for yourself. This subjectivity is the opposite of concentrating
   on divine viewpoint, trusting in God, and focusing on the mission to be accomplished. How do you combat self-pity? The im-
   mature believer enlists the faith-rest drill; the mature believer
   relies on the acquisition of God's happiness. The subsequent
   contentment and tranquillity boost morale and rejuvenate the
   professional attitude of the Christian soldier who might other-
   wise succumb to demoralizing circumstances.

Occupation with Christ further neutralizes preoccupation with self that breeds self-pity. Christ "formed in you [your thinking]" (Gal. 4:19*b*) means He takes precedence in all your considerations. Instead of reacting to people or circumstances with a martyr complex or eliciting pity from those around you, apply the doctrine you have stored. Your soul will relax under pressure and your personal sense of destiny will inspire confidence and courage.

When Bible doctrine becomes your first priority, you ultimately arrive at spiritual self-esteem, personal love for God, the happiness of God, and occupation with Christ. The Apostle Paul describes this pinnacle of the spiritual life.

> For the love of Christ controls [motivates] us.
> (2 Cor. 5:14*a*)

Motivated by the person of Jesus Christ who dwells in you (John 14:20; 17:22–23, 26; Col. 1:27), instead of the fear that inexorably intrudes on your daily life, you find blessing, encouragement, and strength from the inventory of doctrine in your soul. Self-pity arouses only weakness and discouragement. When disaster strikes, you must not seek solace from trouble through panhandling your self-pity; rather you must reflect the serenity of Jesus Christ with whom you are permanently united. Only then will you experience victory over fear.

SPIRITUAL LOGISTICS FOR THE CHRISTIAN SOLDIER

God is perfect, His plan is perfect.[55] But we, the recipients of His plan, are imperfect. Sin devastates our soul, subverting the execution of this plan. Sin is never part of God's purpose for our life. Since carnal Christians cannot execute God's perfect plan, God graciously supplies both the power and the means for overcoming the sins of emotionalism and arrogance, all the human frailties that contradict the protocol plan. When the believer consistently uses the three spiritual skills—the filling of the Holy Spirit, cognition of Bible doctrine through Operation Z,

---

55. The protocol plan of God for the Church is the unique postsalvation spiritual life designed for every believer in the Church Age. See Thieme, *The Divine Outline of History*, 95–97.

and deployment of the ten problem-solving devices—any sin can be defeated before it can interrupt thinking, decisions, and actions.

> For God has not given us a spirit of timidity [fear], but of power [filling of the Spirit] and love [virtue-love] and discipline [sound mind or doctrinal orientation]. (2 Tim. 1:7)

The spiritual life of the mature believer is intimately dependent on virtue-love.[56] Three of the ten problem-solving devices are categorized under virtue-love—personal love for God the Father, impersonal love for all mankind, and occupation with the person of Christ. When virtue-love saturates the soul fear cannot take root. With fear dislodged from the soul the spiritual life flourishes and both courage and common sense become the believer's modus vivendi.

> There is no fear in love; but perfect love [virtue-love] casts out fear. (1 John 4:18a)

The question may be asked, "Do I compromise my spiritual life and defile virtue-love if I kill the enemies of my country in battle?" Definitely not! The spiritual life is compromised only by sin and failure to rebound, never by performing one's duty in combat. When you refuse to allow fear to rule your soul, virtue-love remains intact. Doing your duty in combat does not affect your spiritual life as long as you maintain the filling of the Holy Spirit through rebound and apply problem-solving devices to your combat experience. When you are in God's plan, He works *all* things together for your good—even in combat.

The Christian soldier's first priority is spiritual strength. This spiritual vigor, which promotes battle courage, comes from believing Bible doctrine and applying the ten problem-solving devices. The crippling concerns for personal safety and survival in battle gradually subside. As a believer, your safety is entirely in the hands of the Lord (Ps. 4:8). You will not be removed from this life until the divinely appointed time. Your only concern is to glorify God by executing His protocol plan in your life and in your death.

How do you execute the protocol plan of God? First, you must maintain spirituality through rebound and the filling of the Holy Spirit. Since you have trusted Jesus Christ for the greatest provision—salvation—you can now trust Him for the lesser provision—your daily

---

56. Thieme, *Christian Integrity* (2002), 29–35, 121–50.

needs. By claiming promises with the faith-rest drill you orient to grace. Then, as Bible doctrine becomes the number one priority in your life, it also becomes your entire support system. When you grow spiritually, you acquire humility, a personal sense of destiny, and personal love for God the Father. With spiritual maturity you gain absolute confidence in the Lord, begin to exhibit virtue toward people with impersonal love, and courage toward circumstances. God's happiness settles in your soul to eradicate stress and sustain inner peace. Finally, when you are occupied with Christ by thinking with His mind, you manifest integrity in every situation. Spiritually mature you are part of the pivot—the invisible hero who glorifies God and helps to preserve our client nation.

VICTORY OF THE CHRISTIAN SOLDIER

A serviceman facing the demands of military life generally asks himself two questions:

1. Will I be able to handle the pressures of military life in peace-time or the stress of combat?
2. Will I be killed in battle?

When a believer asks himself these questions, the critical factor affecting his response is the status of his spiritual life.

> According to my earnest expectation and hope [confidence], that I shall not be put to shame in anything, but *that* with all boldness, Christ shall even now, as always, be exalted in my body, whether by life or by death. For to me, to live is Christ, and to die is gain [profit]. (Phil. 1:20–21)

The Apostle Paul expresses spiritual strength as he contemplates his life and eventual death. He views living and dying in terms of his shared destiny and personal relationship with Jesus Christ. If you have spiritual strength from a dynamic spiritual life, you, too, can answer all questions of living and dying with this same assurance. The ten problem-solving devices will bring victory in your life and triumph and dignity to your death.

Victory in Life

The spiritual life begins at the moment of faith alone in Christ alone and continues to the point of physical death. Long before the moment of faith, in eternity past omniscient God decreed a plan for every believer. To live in the framework of that personal plan, believers must exercise their volition to maintain fellowship with God and to make good decisions from divine viewpoint; carnality and human viewpoint propel the believer into bad decisions that distract from God's plan.

The soul of every believer is a battleground. An inner spiritual conflict rages: incessant temptation from the sin nature to make bad decisions from a position of weakness versus the filling of the Holy Spirit who empowers good decisions from the strength of *epignosis* doctrine. Negative volition results in the sin nature's control and loss of spiritual momentum. As carnality continues, the believer becomes entangled in reversionism sinking into moral or immoral degeneracy. Reversionistic Christians become indistinguishable from their unbelieving counterparts. But through positive volition, God the Holy Spirit controls the soul, Bible doctrine permeates the thinking through Operation Z, and the believer progresses into the adult spiritual life becoming a winner in the Christian life.

When you metabolize Bible doctrine, you follow the precedent set by the Lord Himself during His earthly ministry. Through the spiritual life, you, too, can deploy His problem-solving devices plus become occupied with Christ. How will you handle the stress of battle and the pressure of military life? The answer lies with your volition. The decisions you make dictate the life you lead.

LIVING THROUGH COMBAT

Will I survive military service? Does God have a plan for me beyond the war zone? Job 5:19–26 illustrates the response of the mature believer to these questions: Leave the answer in the hands of the Lord.

Job was in agony. He had lost his children and all his possessions. Depressed and despondent he was waiting to die. Although Job was still in the plan of God, Eliphaz, a well meaning but misguided friend, wrongly assumed Job had sinned against God and was under divine discipline. While Eliphaz's false view of the source of Job's suffering caused further testing for Job, Eliphaz does accurately express the certainty that God would solve the problem.

"From six troubles He will deliver you,
Even in seven evil will not touch you." (Job 5:19)

Since God surrounds the believer with a "wall of fire" (Zech. 2:5; 1 Pet. 1:5*a*), we are protected from evil. God constantly converts the evil that assails us to our benefit (Rom. 8:28). As long as we live, God shields and defends us so that we can accomplish His plan.

"Because he [the believer] has loved Me [Jesus Christ],
    therefore I will deliver him;
I will set him *securely* on high, because he has known My
    name.
He will call upon Me, and I will answer him;
I will be with him in trouble;
I will rescue him, and honor him." (Ps. 91:14–15)

What a magnificent message for the Christian soldier in harm's way or for any of us facing adversity. If during the seven greatest pressures of life no evil can defeat the believer in God's plan, how much more will He rescue us from everyday pressures!

Four of these pressures are mentioned in the next two verses; three remain anonymous. The four revealed disasters are famine, war, social disaster, and death. The three unidentified pressures are variables present in the life of every believer. They could be self-induced misery under the law of volitional responsibility, divine discipline for unconfessed sin resulting in punitive action from the Supreme Court of Heaven, or, in the case of the mature believer, suffering for blessing to accelerate spiritual growth.[57] Since this passage warns of future unknown pressures in life, when they surface doctrine will prepare you for them, just as doctrine prepared Job (Job 1:20–22).

"In famine He will redeem [deliver] you from death,
And in war from the power of the sword." (Job 5:20)

In Job's era famine was synonymous with economic recession, depression, or disaster. God promises to rescue His people from malnourishment and starvation. This same promise that applied in the time of

---

57. Thieme, *Christian Suffering* (2002), 62–67.

Job also applies to believers in Jesus Christ today. No matter how great the economic calamity, until God's plan for that believer is completed he will survive the adversity. Understanding God's plan from Bible doctrine launches the faith-rest drill and consolidates a personal sense of destiny—the certainty of a future in time and eternity.

The second disaster reveals God's design for the Christian soldier. In battle or under combat pressure you will be protected from "the power of the sword." No weapon of war, no matter how destructive, will take your life as long as God's plan calls for you to remain on earth. "The battle is the Lord's" (1 Sam. 17:47b).

"You will be hidden from the scourge of the tongue [social disaster],
Neither will you be afraid of violence [death] when it comes." (Job 5:21)

When you are the victim of character assassination—slander, gossip, maligning, judging—social disaster can attain monumental proportions. Sins of the tongue are devastating, but the Lord will protect you from malicious defamation. He will strengthen and vindicate you against the most vicious of verbal assaults (Isa. 54:17; Rom. 14:4). The Lord judges with intense discipline those who judge and defame (Matt. 7:1–2; Rom. 2:1). God also protects from the fourth adversity, so that when violence and death threaten, you need not fear. You cannot be removed from this life apart from the sovereign decision of a wise and loving God.

In the next paragraph, Job 5:22–26, violence and death are mentioned in some detail.

"You will laugh at violence [death] and famine [economic disaster]." (Job 5:22a)

To have a sense of humor, to have a relaxed mental attitude under the horrendous pressures of life, to be able to respond to inordinate disaster by using the ten problem-solving devices—this is what is meant by "you will laugh at violence and famine." Laughing indicates inner contentment and tranquillity amidst overwhelming catastrophe. The believer with serenity and a sense of humor derived from sharing God's happiness thrives under the pressures of life.

"Neither will you be afraid of wild beasts." (Job 5:22b)

In the ancient world wild beasts often attacked vulnerable and un-suspecting persons who perished from their injuries. Therefore, in this context "wild beast" is a metaphor for sudden, violent catastrophe. When facing brutal conditions, courage from Bible doctrine results in an attitude that is prepared for anything, yet relaxed. The believer knows that all the 'wild beasts' in this world cannot menace or ruin him. He is not intimidated by the proximity of upheaval and devastation. He is calm, secure in his dependence on divine safekeeping.

> "For you will be in league [alliance] with the stones of
> the field;
> And the beasts of the field will be at peace with you."
> (Job 5:23)

In conclusion Eliphaz assures of divine protection from the stones that were used as ammunition for an ancient weapon—the sling. Today that ordnance includes rifle bullets, artillery rounds, missiles, or other lethal projectiles. You are allied with the ammunition meant for your destruction. In other words, no bullet has your name on it as long as the Lord has a plan for your life. You can be at ease in a hostile environment because the Lord has allotted your moment for dying and no destructive device can remove you from this earth until that time. When His plan for you is completed, dying is profit.

Job 5:24 continues the conclusion addressing our mental and physical well-being despite the seven disasters of life.

> "And you will know that your tent is secure,
> For you will visit your abode and fear no loss." (Job 5:24)

As Job sat on the ground for seven days and seven nights (Job 2:13) overwhelmed by disaster with nothing left but his integrity, how ironic that Eliphaz should mention Job's "tent" as being "secure." From the human viewpoint nothing in Job's life seemed secure. Yet Job had security. Without God's permission, nothing could harm Job or his property, remove him from this earth (Job 2:6), or shake the foundations of his relaxed mental attitude. Likewise, your tranquillity and life remain secure even if encountering a hail of gunfire or a barrage of high explosive shells. When the time does come for you to be absent from the body and face to face with the Lord—a place of no more sorrow, no more pain, no more death, you will arrive in heaven, an abode of everlasting, perfect happiness, to await the resurrection (2 Cor. 5:8; Rev. 21:4).

"You will know also that your descendants will be many,
And your offspring as the grass of the earth." (Job 5:25)

The principle enucleated in this verse affirms that life must go on.
Even if you die in combat, God's plan for the lives of those left behind
and His plan for the advance of history does not stop. You should know
that personal blessing will continue to be extended to all your loved ones.

At first Job 5:25 appears to mean that you will have numerous children who will multiply prolifically, but the scope is much broader—all
human life will continue. God guarantees the survival of the human race
in spite of mankind's propensity for self-destruction. As an extension of
the prehistoric angelic conflict, the human chronicle will continue until
Satan's sentence is executed at the end of the Millennium (Rev. 20:10;
cf., 2 Pet. 3:7, 10). Since the Millennium is still future, the destruction
of mankind by nuclear holocaust, environmental disaster, or any other
worldwide catastrophe is not only pure fiction but humanly impossible.
Only the Lord Jesus Christ Himself at the close of the Millennium will
destroy the present universe and create "a new heaven and a new earth."
There all believers will dwell for all eternity (2 Pet. 3:10–13; Rev. 21:1).

"You will come to the grave in full vigor,
Like the stacking of grain in its season." (Job 5:26)

This verse is the epilogue of the Eliphaz discourse dedicated to
those in uniform who may face death in combat. The agricultural
metaphor of "the stacking of grain in its season" reveals a right and a
wrong time for harvest. Only an expert can determine the right time.
In all matters of life and death timing is critical and God is the expert.

The "season" for your death is not determined by your age or
human volition but by the sovereignty, love, and wisdom of God.
"Stacking of grain" is analogous to your soul and spirit departing from
this body of corruption in physical death and transferring to heaven.
Since God stacks the grain at the right time, your death is God's victory; whether on a battlefield or in bed, whether in youth or old age,
death is always God's call.

Victory over Death

Will you die in combat? Since death is in God's hands, you can
eliminate it from your list of worries. Neither the threat of violence

nor any form of deadly weapon can remove you from this life until the Lord so allows. Your demise is strictly the decision of God. You have no control as to the time, the manner, or the place of death. Death is the sovereign decision of God's infallible wisdom, impeccable integrity, and unfailing love for you as a member of Christ's royal family. God's perfect justice and righteousness guarantee that He is absolutely fair in His decision regarding your death. You never need to question His wisdom concerning your departure or the loss of a loved one. While volition is a determining factor in how you live, the sovereignty of God is the determining factor when you die. How well you die when the time comes for the Lord to take you home depends on your spiritual life.

Since death is an expression of God's will and He desires only the best for the believer, dying is gain [profit]. Why? Because every believer gains infinitely more in eternity than the wealthiest, most powerful, most privileged person who has ever lived.

Numerous passages in the Word of God instruct the believer not to fear death. Death for the believer is going to sleep, and who is afraid to go to sleep? Death is going home, and who is afraid to go home? Death is arriving face to face with the Lord, and who is afraid to be face to face with the Lord? Death is God's victory. Whether you are carnal or spiritual, a winner or loser believer, in spiritual maturity or Christian degeneracy, your death will always be His triumph.

> "O DEATH, WHERE IS YOUR VICTORY? O DEATH, WHERE IS YOUR STING?". . . But thanks be to God, who gives us the victory through our Lord Jesus Christ." (1 Cor. 15:55, 57)

> Precious in the sight of the LORD
> Is the death of His godly ones [believers]. (Ps. 116:15)

> "The LORD gave [life] and the LORD has taken away [death].
> Blessed be the name of the Lord." (Job 1:21*b*)

Six principles summarize the concept of victory over death.

1. Since the believer's death is strictly God's decision, the Lord's will for us always embraces victory.
2. The divine decision regarding the believer's death includes the time, the manner, the place of death. Therefore, nothing can remove the believer from this life except God.

3. Since God is perfect, His timing is perfect in all matters of life and death for the believer. No believer in God's plan can die prematurely.

4. Death is the wise and gracious choice of God and is always in the best interest of the believer. Therefore, none of us has the right to question God's perfect wisdom.

5. No circumstances, not even warfare, can remove the believer from this life without divine consent. The believer is always under God's protection.

6. In death we are absent from the body and face to face with the Lord. We are in a place of perfect happiness.

"And He shall wipe away every tear from their eyes; and there shall no longer be *any* death; there shall no longer be *any* mourning, or crying, or pain; the first things [the mortal or living phase] have passed away." (Rev. 21:4)

Victory over Sorrow

But we do not want you to be uninformed, brethren, about those who are asleep, that you may not grieve, as do the rest who have no hope. (1 Thess. 4:13)

"Brethren . . . who are asleep" is a metaphor for Christian death and reminds all believers of their mortality. Apart from the Rapture generation we will all experience physical death. In Christ we do not despair over our losses as do unbelievers who have no hope. Our hope in the Lord Jesus Christ is the confidence that we will all be resurrected on that imminent day of His return. For the Lord Himself said at a grave side,

"I am the resurrection and the life; he who believes in Me shall live even if he dies." (John 11:25*b*)

Enduring grief becomes an imperative of the Christian life because we will be resurrected and reunited with our loved ones in heaven. Our eternal future with the Lord Jesus Christ is secure. However, our immediate future may hold many bombshells—there is every possibility of war, disaster, sudden death. We must ask ourselves: Do we have the resources to carry grief with grace and poise, to fulfill the noble purpose for which we are called by the Lord?

If you lose someone in the service of the nation, recall the grace of God in your bereavement. Although memories of the dearly departed stir sorrow and tenderness, remember that those who have died in Christ are now in a place of no more sorrow, tears, pain, or death—a residence in heaven so wonderful that the description of its glory cannot be comprehended by mortal man. With the assurance that your believing loved ones are securely in the hands of the Lord in eternal happiness and perfect contentment, you can press on and continue living your life as unto the Lord. Remember these important principles as you mourn those you love.

1. You cannot stop normal living because people you love have died and gone to heaven.
2. You cannot resent others who are enjoying life when you are in a state of sorrow.
3. You cannot demand that your friends or fellow Christians alter their lives to join you in extended mourning and grief.

Although you are emotionally involved in the death of a loved one and your grief continues, you should understand a principle: You must not tarnish the memory of their death by becoming morbid, resentful, bitter, or vindictive, especially against others who may not share in your pain and grief. Even though your heartache is intensely personal and you will remember long after others forget, you must release your friends to go on living. Take comfort from Bible doctrine that in death your loved one has entered into exalted blessings. In this way you will fulfill the encouragement of Job 5:25 to continue your life, not in a callous way but in a tender way, recognizing what God does for those who die.

You will not resent the laughter, the happiness of others who are not in the midst of heartache. You must go on living and let your grief be a private matter between you and the Lord. Your loneliness and sorrow belong to you, as does the fragrance of memories. Confidence belongs to you because you have learned to apply the Word of God through the ten problem-solving devices. Comfort belongs to you knowing that your believing loved ones dwell in heaven. What does *not* belong to you are resentment, bitterness, and hatred toward those who do not seem to care.

Occupation with Christ focuses your thoughts on the Lord, not on your anguish—you can tenderly remember those who have died but you must carry on. You keep on living, learning, and applying Bible doctrine so when you reach occupation with Christ, you can experience what your loved ones who have gone before you already know: Living is Christ, and dying is profit.

In my soul I carry sorrow for loved ones who have died—family, friends, various associates, extraordinary people I have known in the past. Since I am of the World War II generation, numerous close friends from childhood and from those war years are gone. I honor them through my fragrance of memories of our times together. My life does not cease because they are no longer here. I cannot resign my responsibility to study and teach the Word of God because I retain a deep sadness for those I loved. It would be dishonoring to their memory to retreat into a prolonged melancholy. I cannot impose such sorrow on others by arrogantly insisting they share my grief. But I can tell you how I have handled my own grief.

"F" FOR FREDDIE

Charles Frederick McIntosh was my first Christian friend after I became a believer and was one of the closest friends of my life. We were inseparable until the time I went to college at the University of Arizona and he went to UCLA. During the summers I lifeguarded on Catalina Island and he worked nearby so we saw each other frequently.

He was a wonderful believer with the spiritual gift of pastor-teacher. I have never heard anyone communicate the Scriptures in such a marvelous way. People would sit and listen with rapt attention as he gave a testimony or a message of Bible doctrine.

When Pearl Harbor was attacked and the United States entered World War II, I had been an officer in service for about a year. Freddie had just graduated from UCLA and went on to join the Army Air Corps where he became a flying cadet. After graduation "F" for Freddie was sent to the European theater. Before shipping overseas he visited the headquarters where I was stationed to say good-bye. One of the last things I said to him was, "Freddie, you are going to come back with an exciting repertoire of illustrations for your ministry after the war."

I remember the letters Freddie wrote, not about his heroism, although he was highly decorated, but about those men with whom he served. He was the pilot of a B-17 with a crew of ten. He asked me to pray for his crew members. He wrote every time one accepted Christ as Savior. I think the navigator was the first, then the bombardier, then the tail-gunner. His final letter came just prior to his twenty-fifth mission confirming that every person in his air crew was a believer in Jesus Christ.

On that twenty-fifth mission which was over Berlin the starboard engines were hit by flak and caught fire. Freddie manually held the B-17 in position so his crew could bail out. When he gave the order to jump, the navigator asked, "Are you coming with us?" Freddie replied, "I will when I can." The navigator was the last to exit the crippled bomber. As his parachute opened, he looked up and saw the aircraft engulfed in flames. A massive explosion tore through the fuselage and Freddie McIntosh went into eternity.

When I received word of Freddie's death, I was shocked and grief-stricken. Not only was he my best friend but he had such splendid plans for a postwar ministry. Yet the Lord took him home. I had some difficult times dealing with his death. Many nights, especially when I was on duty with the Air Force, I would go out to watch a few planes come in and remember Fred. I would give him a salute and then leave. Remembering was truly sad for me. In time, however, I came to understand the doctrine I am now communicating to you.

Some of you in the near or distant future will face the death of someone you hold dear. You now have the information to handle that situation. The rest is up to you. There is no substitute for daily perception of Bible doctrine in overcoming grief. Through the application of doctrine, you can be at peace when the Lord takes someone home to be with Himself.

TRIBUTE TO THE NOBLE WARRIOR

Like salvation, freedom is a gift purchased at an enormous cost. Brave soldiers pay with their lives on battlefields all over the world so we might live in freedom. A most poignant homage to their courage and nobility was articulated by General of the Army Douglas MacArthur in Los Angeles, 26 January 1955, at the dedication ceremony of a monument erected in his honor. His eloquent description is a worthy tribute to those who sacrifice themselves on the altar of our country.

I have listened with deep emotion to these solemn proceedings and my heart is too full for my lips to express adequately my thanks and appreciation for the extraordinary honor you do me.

Even so, I understand full well that this memorial is intended to commemorate an epoch rather than an individual; an armed force rather than its commander; a nation rather than its servant; an ideal rather than a personality. This but increases my pride, that my name has been the one chosen as the symbol of an epic struggle and victory by millions of unnamed others. It is their heroism, their sacrifice, their success, that you have honored today in so unforgettable a manner. I, and this statue, and this park are but the selected reminders of their grandeur. Most of them were citizen soldiers, sailors and airmen—men from the farm, from the city, from the schoolroom, from the college campus—men not dedicated to the profession of arms, men not primarily skilled in the arts of destruction—men amazingly like the men you see and meet and know each day of your lives—but men animated, inspired and ennobled by a sublime cause—the defense of their country, of their native land, of their very hearthstones. The most divine of all human sentiments and impulses guided them—the spirit and willingness to sacrifice. He who dares to die—to lay his life on the altar of his nations's need—is beyond doubt the noblest development of mankind. In this he comes closest to the image of his Creator who died on the cross that the human soul might live.

These men were my comrades-in-arms. With me they knew the far call of the bugles at reveille; the distant roll of the drums at nightfall; the endless tramp of marching feet; the incessant whine of sniper bullets; the ceaseless rattle of sputtering machine guns; the ominous roar of threatening cannon; the sinister wail of air sirens; the deafening blasts of crashing bombs; the stealthy stroke of hidden torpedoes; the amphibious lurch over perilous waves; the dark majesty of fighting ships; the mad din of battle lines; and all the stench and ghastly horror and savage destruction of a stricken area of war. They suffered hunger and thirst; the broiling suns of relentless heat; the torrential rains of tropical storms; the loneliness and utter desolation of jungle trails; the bitterness of separation from those they loved and cherished. They went on, and on, and on, when everything within them seemed to stop and die. They grew old in youth. They burned out in searing minutes all that life owed them of tranquil years. When I think of their patience under adversity, of their courage under fire, and of their modesty in victory, I am filled with an emotion of admiration I cannot express. Many of them trod the tragic path of unknown fame that led to a stark white cross above a lonely grave. And from their tortured, dying lips, with the dreadful gurgle of the death rattle in their throats, always came the same gasping prayer that we who were left would go on to victory. I do not know the dignity of their birth, but I do know the glory of their death, and I am sure a merciful God has taken them unto Himself.

Their sacrifice for our cherished liberty inspires and heartens the souls of all who remember. Just as the Lord Jesus Christ made the greatest sacrifice of all history on the cross—dying so that mankind might have eternal life—so the soldier sacrifices his time, his fortune, and sometimes his life that others might live in freedom. For those of us who are the beneficiaries of these two majestic sacrifices, let us never forget the honor due our Lord and Savior Jesus Christ and the intrepid men who purchase freedom through military victory.

Glossary

age of accountability The point of God-consciousness when a person recognizes the possibility of the existence of a supreme being and is able to understand the Gospel. From this moment each individual is responsible to God for positive and negative volition.

angelic conflict The unseen invisible warfare between God and Satan, ignited by Satan's prehistoric revolution. When God sentenced Satan to eternal judgment, Satan appealed the sentence, accusing God of injustice; God responded by creating the human race to resolve the angelic conflict, demonstrating His perfect integrity and grace in human history despite satanic opposition.

Armageddon The last battle of the last campaign of the last war of human history that takes place on the plain of Esdraelon near the city of Megiddo in which the forces of the returned Lord Jesus Christ defeat the forces of gentile empires mobilized to annihilate Israel.

categories The hermeneutical principle of comparing Scripture with Scripture to determine the classification of doctrine.

Church Age The current dispensation of human history which began on the day of Pentecost (A.D. 30), fifty days after the crucifixion of Jesus Christ, and terminates with the resurrection or the Rapture of the Church.

client nation A national entity in which a certain number of spiritually mature believers have formed a pivot sufficient to sustain the nation and through which God furthers His plan for mankind. Under divine blessing God specifically protects this representative nation so believers can fulfill the divine mandates of evangelism, communication and custodianship of Bible doctrine, and sending missionaries abroad.

divine establishment, laws of Principles ordained by God for the survival, stability, protection, and perpetuation of the human race, believers and unbelievers alike, during human history.

divine institutions Four founding principles for all mankind ordained by God and governed by the laws of divine establishment for the perpetuation, stability, protection, and freedom of the human race: 1. the individual; 2. marriage; 3. family; 4. the national entity. Each institution is regulated by a corresponding authority: 1. volition; 2. husband; 3. parents; 4. government.

faith-rest The believer's basic technique for claiming the promises of God and mixing them with faith to generate tranquility of soul in the midst of the adversities or prosperities of life.

fifth cycle of discipline Destruction of a nation as a result of apostasy, the maximum rejection of biblical principles.

FLOT A military acronym for 'Forward Line Of Troops' used as an acrostic for the divine defense line of problem-solving devices formed from Bible doctrine circulating in the right lobe of the soul; God's protection for the believer against invasion by all the insidious enemies of the spiritual life.

isagogics The interpretation of Scripture within the framework of its historical setting or prophetical environment.

Millennium A literal period of one thousand years beginning after the Second Advent of Jesus Christ in which He will fulfill all unconditional covenants to Israel, reign on the throne of David, and establish worldwide peace and perfect environment.

pivot Mature believers living within a national entity whose spiritual advance establishes client nation status and guarantees its perpetuation in every generation. These invisible heroes provide the prosperity and preservation of that nation through blessing by association.

problem-solving devices Ten divine solutions available to every advancing believer; the aggregate of all that God provides for the Church Age believer to accomplish His plan and to glorify Him; the only means by which Bible doctrine can be applied in the life of the believer. Every human problem can be solved through employing these ten devices: rebound, the filling of the Holy Spirit, the faith-rest drill, grace orientation, doctrinal orientation, a personal sense of destiny, personal love for God the Father, impersonal love for all mankind, sharing the happiness of God, and occupation with Christ.

Rapture The resurrection of all living and dead Church Age believers from the earth to meet the Lord in the air and become the Bride of Christ. The Rapture takes place at the end of the Church Age immediately before the Tribulation begins.

rebound The grace provision for the carnal believer to recover the filling of the Holy Spirit through naming personal sins privately to God the Father; the method of restoring the believer's fellowship with God to resume the spiritual life.

regeneration Spiritual birth or being "born again" that occurs at the moment of salvation.

sin nature The center of man's rebellion toward God. The sin nature is transferred genetically as a direct result of Adam's first sin, and thereafter resides in the cell structure of the human body of every human being except Jesus Christ.

Tribulation A period of seven literal years which completes the Age of Israel, immediately following the Rapture of the Church and terminating with the Second Advent of Christ.

virtue-love A nonemotional motivation of the soul acquired through the filling of the Holy Spirit and maximum doctrine in the soul. Virtue-love is manifested in personal love for God and impersonal love for all mankind. It is a mental attitude that characterizes the spiritually mature believer who has integrity and capacity for life, happiness, and personal love relationships.

volitional responsibility The divine law that holds every human being accountable for his decisions and actions before the Supreme Court of Heaven.

Yahweh The Lord was revealed in the Old Testament under the sacred Tetragrammaton יהוה. *Yahweh* or Jehovah was the name by which Israel identified the Second Person of the Trinity. In other contexts, *Yahweh* refers to God the Father or the Holy Spirit. Out of reverence the Jews never pronounced this name; instead, the Lord was called *Adonai*.

Scripture Index

OLD TESTAMENT

NEW TESTAMENT

Subject Index